Dictionary of Computer Science and Engineering

notionpress.com

Dictionary of Computer Science and Engineering

HemaKumar G
Dr. Punitha P

notionpress.com

Notion Press

5 Muthu Kalathy Street, Triplicane,

Chennai - 600 005

First Published by Notion Press 2014

ISBN: 978-93-84049-52-2

16-Bit A processer which handle data in 16-bits words, providing much faster operation than older eight-bit systems.

32-Bit System A processor that is capable of Handing 32-bit data.

A

A* Search Algorithm The A* algorithm is a specialization of best-first search. It provides general guidelines with which to estimate goal distances for general search graphs.

Place the starting node s on open.

If open is empty, stop and return failure.

Remove from open the node n that has the smallest value of f*(n). If the node is a goal node, return success and stop. Otherwise,

Expand n, generating all of its successor's n' and place n on closes. For every successor n', if n' is not already on open or closed attach a back-pointer to n, compute f*(n) and place it on open.

Each n' that is already open or closed should be attached to back pointers which reflect the lowest g*(n') path. If n' was on closed and its pointer was changed, remove it and place it on open.

Return to step 2.

Absolute Absolute (of a value) real and unchanging. For example,

An absolute address is a location in memory and an absolutes cell reference is a single fixed cell in a Spread sheet display. The opposite of absolute is Relative.

Abstract Class An abstract class is a class that has no direct instances but whose descendent classes have direct instances.

Accelerator Board Expansion board that makes a computer run faster, It Usually contains an additional central processing unit.

Accelerator Card A method of speeding up an old PC by replacing the existing processor chip with a special add-in card that has a newer, faster processor.

Accelerator Key A combination of keys that, when pressed together, carry out a task that you would have to select from a menu using a mouse. For example, instead of selecting the File menu then the Save option, many programs let you the accelerator keys Alt and S to do the same thing and save the file.

Access The way, in which the file access is provided, so that the data can be stored retrieved or updated by the computer.

Access Time Access time or reaction time, the time taken by a computer, after an instruction has been given to read from or write to memory.

Account Your subscription to a networked computer system.

Account Name Same as your login ID, user ID. The word type at the "Login:" prompts; your electronic name.

Accumulator A special register or memory location in the arithmetic and logic unit of the computer processor. It is used to hold the result of a calculation temporarily or to store data that is being transferred.

Accumulator Register This register holds the initial data to be operated upon, the intermediate results, and also the final results of processing operations. It is used during the executions of most instructions. The results of arithmetic operations are returned to the accumulator register for transfer to main storage through the memory buffer register. In many computers there are more than one accumulator registers.

A

Accuracy The precision of computations and control.

Acoustic Coupler A type of modem that has rubber cups that fit on the mouth and earpiece of a normal phone. This converts data from the PC into sound that is then transmitted across the phone network to another computer with a modem. Most modems plug directly into a telephone socket and provide quality sound, which means that they are more reliable. An Acoustic Coupler sends data more slowly than a modem. But it is useful if you are travelling and need to use public or hotel telephones to send data.

Acoustic Coupler Device Acoustic coupler device that enable computer data to be transmitted and received through a normal telephone handset; the handset rests on coupler to make the connection. A small speaker within the device is used to convert the computer's digital output data into analogue sound signals, which are then picked up by the handset and transmitted through the telephone system. At the receiving telephone, a second acoustic coupler or modem converts the sound signals back into digital data for input into a computer. Unlike a modem, an acoustic coupler does not require direct connection to the telephone system.

Acrobat Coding Acrobat coding system developed by Adobe systems for electronic publishing application. Acrobat coding can be generated directly from postscript files.

Acronym Acronym word formed from the initial letters and/ or syllables of other words, intended as a pronounceable abbreviation- for example ADC, ADA so on.

Active Window The section of a screen that is currently being used. In Microsoft Windows, the active window is in front of any other window and has its title bar (at the top of the window) colored blue. Windows which are displayed but which are not active have a white bar.

Activex Controls An ActiveX control is an object that supports a customizable, programmatic interface. Examples of ActiveX Controls include text boxes, command buttons, audio players, video players, stock tickets and so on. You can develop ActiveX Controls using Microsoft Visual Basic, Java and Microsoft Visual C++.

Ada ADA high-level computer-programming language developed and owned by the US Department directly of controls a process or machine, such as a military aircraft, The language took more than five years to specify and become commercially available only in the late 1980s. It is named after English mathematician Ada Augusta Byron.

Adaline Acronym for a linear neuron: ADAptive LINear Element.

Adapter Card That plugs into an expansion bus in a PC and adds a new function to the computer, or allows it to communicate with another device. For example, a sound card is a type of adapter card that plugs into an expansion connector and allows sound to be played back or recorded.

Adaption Training method that proceeds through the specified sequence of inputs, calculating the output, error, and network adjustment for each input vector in the sequence as the inputs are presented.

A

Adaptive Filter Network that contains delays and whose weights are adjusted after each new input vector is presented. The network adapts to changes in the input signal properties if such occur. This kind of filter is used in long distance telephone lines to cancel echoes.

Adaptive Learning Rate Learning rate that is adjusted according to an algorithm during training to minimize training time.

Adc Analogue to digital converter.

Adder Adder electronic circuit in a computer or calculator that carries out the process of adding each pair of binary bits, such circuit are essential components of a computer's arithmetic and logic unit (ALU).

Address Like a postal address, a "network address" is used to locate another user for the purpose of directing mail. On the Internet this is in the form: account@host.domain.

Address Calculation Sort (Hashing) In this method a function f is applied to each key.

The result of this function determines into which of the several sub-files the record is to be placed.

The function should have the property that: if x <= y, f (x) <= f (y), Such a function is called order preserving.

An item is placed into a sub-file in correct sequence by placing sorting method – simple insertion is often used.

Addressing Modes Early every instruction involves one or two operands. The operand may be register, immediate data (constants) or memory operands (variables). The way an instruction references its operands, is called its addressing modes, which may be of the three basic types: Register, Immediate and Memory.

Advanced Scsi Programming Interface	A software standard that allows a SCSI controller to communicate other software.
Agent	The part of a system that performs information preparation and exchange on behalf of an application.
Aggregation	Aggregation is the "part-whole" or "a-part-of" relationship in which objects representing the components of something are associated with an object representing the entire assembly. For example, a name, argument list, and a compound statement are part of a C-language function definition, which in turn is part of an entire program. Aggregation is a tightly coupled form of association with some extra semantics. The most significant property of aggregation is transitivity, that is, if A is part of B and B is part of C, then A is part of C. aggregation is also anti-symmetric, that is, if A is part of B, then B is not part of A. finally, some properties of the assembly propagate to the components as well, possibly with some local modifications.
Ai & Cognitive Science	Researchers from AI & psychology have joined together to some universities to form a separate discipline known as cognitive science. Like AI researchers, cognitive scientists are interested in the computation processes required to perform certain human functions & in the mental & computational states related to such processes like computer science, cognitive science is still searching for a theory & foundation that will qualify it as a science.

A

AI & EE (Electrical Engineering)	AI has much in common with engineering particularly electrical and mechanical engineering. AI & EE are both interested in computational processes and systems, and how they relate to senses of perception such as vision and speech.
AI & Linguistics	The field of linguistics shares an interest in the theory of grammars & languages with AI. Both fields have a desire to build a well-founded theory, & to see the development of systems that understand natural languages, that can synthesize speech & that are capable of language translations.
AI & ME (Mechanical Engineering)	They share common interests in their desire to build intelligent robots. Their goals are to build robots that can see & move around, perform mechanical tasks and understand human speech.
AI & Psychologists	They are concerned with workings of mind, the mental and emotional processes that drive human behavior. As such, we should not be surprised to learn that researchers in AI have much in common with psychologists during last 20 years. AI has adopted models of thinking & learning form psychology. AI has given psychologists fresh ideas and enhances their ability to model human cognitive functions as computer.
AI & Related Fields	AI is closely related with fields like engineering, particularly Electrical and Mechanical Engineering, Linguistics, Psychology, Cognitive science and Philosophy. Robotics is also regarded by some researchers as a branch of AI but this view is not common.

AI & Robotics Robotics is also related with AI by some researches. They said it is a branch of AI but this view is not common. Because many researcher consider robotics as a separate inter disciplinary field which combines concepts & techniques from AI, electrical & mechanical & optical engineering.

ALGOI ALGOI (acronym for algorithmic language) early high-level programming language, developed in the 1950s and 1960s for Scientific applications. A general-purpose language, Although no longer in common use it his greatly influenced more recent languages, such as ADA and PASCAL and get type of logic gate.

Algorithm Consists of a set of explicit and unambiguous finite steps which, when carried out for a given set of initial conditions, produce the corresponding output & terminate in a finite time. A method or procedure that solves a particular problem or performs some desired task. Programmers write instructions to implement particular algorithms in their programs. The choice of algorithm affects the performance, memory requirements and so forth.

Alias A type of nickname (usually short and easy to remember) that refers to a type of network resource. Aliases are used so you won't have to remember the long and difficult names typical of network resource.

Align To line up text so that either the left or right-hand margin is level. If text is left aligned, all the characters line up on left-hand side, but don't on the right-hand side. If text is justified then the text lines up on left-and right-hand edges.

A

Alpha Test	It is conducted at the developers' site by a customer. The software is used in a natural setting with the developer "Looking over the shoulder" of the user and recording errors and usage problems. Alpha tests are conducted in a controlled environment.
Alt Key	A key on a PC's keyboard used to activate special functions in a program. The Alt key has become the standard method of bringing up the menu bar in any software running on a PC. For example, Alt-F normally displays the File menu of a program; Alt-X normally exits the program.
Alternate Key	A candidate key that is not the primary key is called an alternate key.
Analog	A method of storing information, used by most audiotapes, Videotapes and laser discs. An analog device uses a physical quantity, such as length or voltage, to represent the value of a number. By contrast, digital storage relies on a coding system of numeric units.
Anonymous FTP	By using the word "anonymous" as your user ID and your email address as the password when you login to an FTP site, you can bypass local security checks and gain limited access to public files on the remote computer. This type of access is available on most FTP sites, but not all.
ANSI	American National Standards Institute.
Anti-Aliasing	A technique used to reduce the jagged edges that appear when circles or curves are displayed or printed out. Anti-aliasing fills this gap with a shade of the color so the eye blends these together to give the impression of a smooth curve.

AO* Algorithm It is basically used to find the minimum cost solution tree if one exists.

Place the start node s on open.

Using the search tree constructed thus for, compute the most promising solution tree T_0.

Select a node n that is both an open and a part of T_0. Remove n from open and place it is closed.

If n is a terminal goal node, label n as solved. If the solution of n results in any of n's ancestors being solved, label all the ancestors as solved. If the start node s is solved, exit with success where T_0 is the solution tree. Remove from open all nodes with a solved ancestor.

If n is not a solvable node, label n as unsolvable. If the start node is labeled as unsolvable, exit with failure. If any of n's ancestors become unsolvable because n is, label then unsolvable as well remove from open all nodes with unsolvable ancestors.

Otherwise, expand node n generating all of its successors. For each such successor node that contains more than one sub-problem, generate their successor's to give individual sub-programs. Attach to each newly generated node a back pointer to its predecessor compute the cost estimate h* at n and each ancestor of n.

Return to step 2.

API Applications Program Interface.

Application Sometimes known as a client or an "app" it's a program that performs a specific function. FTP, Mail, Gopher, Mosaic, and Telnet clients are the most common examples of internet application.

A

Application Development The process of combing and arranging computer routines to create a program designed for a particular use. Application development programs or systems complete with standard routines are designed to simplify the process of creating applications, eliminating the need to program each new application form scratch.

Application Generator A feature if some computer programs that assists the user with a program designed to create custom applications. In some cases, the application can be made a standard-alone utility that does not require the full program to run.

Application Program A computer software package used to perform a variety of related tasks such as for accounting, word processing, desktop publishing, etc.

Application Programming Language Application programs are designed for specific computer applications, such as payroll processing, inventory control etc. to write programs for payroll processing or other applications, the programmer does not need to control the basic circuitry of a computer. Instead the programmer needs that make it easy to input data, produce output, do calculations, store and retrieve data.

Archie Archie is a way of automatically gathering, indexing and sometimes even retrieving files on the Internet. Most good Archie clients are able to FTP files once you've found the information you're looking for.

Architecture The design of a computer that defines such things as type of processor, transfer speed, bus size, etc.

Architecture Description of the number of the layers in a neural network, each layer's transfer function, the number of neurons per layer, and the connections between layers.

Archive A collection of files stored on an Internet machine. FTP sites are known as archives.

Artificial Intelligence (AI) Descriptive of the ability of a computer to simulate human intelligence, as by recording corrections to its output adjusting for future transactions.

AI is a branch of computer science which deals with the study and creation of computer system that show some form of intelligence systems that learn new concepts and tasks, systems that can understand a natural language or perceive and comprehend and systems that perform other types of facts that require human types of intelligence.

Artificial Language A computer programming language with a distinct set of rules and vocabulary.

ASA American Standard Association.

ASAD Association of Share Authors and Distributors.

ASCII Stands for American Standard Code for Information Inter-change and is pronounced as key. This is a numerical code used to represent characters. For example, A is 65 and B is 66. ASCII is used by almost all computers, software and comms system, allowing different computers to exchange data. ASCII is not completely standardized. The first 128 characters are well defined and normally adhered to and cover letters, numbers and simple controls such as Delete. The characters between 128 and the limit of ASCII, 255, are far from standard.

A

Assembler Directives (Pseudo Op-Code) Neither represents machine instruction to be included in the object nor indicates the allocation of storage for constants or program variables. These statements direct the assemblers to take certain action during the process of assembling the program. They are also used to indicate certain things regarding how assembly of the input program to be performed.

Assembly Language An assembly language is a lowest level programming language for a computer. It is peculiar for a certain computer system and is hence machine dependent.

Associative Networks It is directed graphs with labeled nodes and arcs or arrows. The language used in constructing a network is based on selected domain primitives for objects and relations as well as some general primitives.

Associative network structure is used in the matching techniques. It is also known as semantic networks.

Asynchronous Transfer Mode A transfer method that dynamically allocates bandwidth using a fixed-size packet, or cell. Also known as fast packet.

Asynchronous Communication The recognition and transmission of date as it becomes available rather than at timed intervals. Asynchronous communication is more or less continuous because data is transmitted as it becomes available without the constraints of a timing device.

ATL (Active Template Library) It provides the mechanism to use and create Component Object Model objects. ATL is the Active Template Library, a set of template-based C++ classes with which you can easily create small, fast Component Object Model (COM) objects. It has special support for key COM features including: stock implementations of Unknown, IClassFactory, IClassFactory2 and IDispatch; dual interfaces; standard COM enumerator interfaces; connection point; tear-off interfaces; and Dispatch dual interfaces; standard COM enumerator interfaces; connection points; tear-off interface ActiveX controls.

ATM (Asynchronous Transfer Mode) ATM scheme is widely used for data communication in telecommunication network. An ATM network use an ATM switches receives the request for data transfer from different computers. The ATM switch facilitates the data transfer in asynchronous mode. The ATM switch connects the sender's and receivers computers and transfers the packets to destination at a high speed.

ATN (Augmented Transition Network) ATN is a versatile Network. The ATN includes tests actions as parts of the are components & special registers to help in building syntactic structures with a ATN, Extensive semantic analysis is even possible & using the register contents, an ATN builds a partial structural description of the sentence as it moves from state to state in network.

Audibility The ease with which conformance to standards can be checked.

A

Audio File	A file that contains digital sample data from a sound. In windows, audio files normally have a .WAV extension and are played back or recorded using the Sound Recorder utility in the Accessories group.
Audio/Video Interleaved (AVI)	Standard that describes how video frames and simultaneous sound should be stored in a single file. In a PC, these files have an AVI extension and can be played back using the Media Player utility in the Accessories group.
Augmented Backus – Naur Form(ABNF)	A way of writing grammars that complies with the SRGS standard. It is a fairly simple and very human–readable format.
Authentication	Any process that ensures that users are who they say they are. When you type your name and password, you are authenticated and allowed access.
Automatic Backup	A program feature that creates a backup copy of a file each time changes are saved. A program or routine that backup data in the computer at a predetermined time, usually set to operate at the end of the day or during other off hours.

B

B$^+$ Tree File Structure The B$^+$ tree file structure is the most widely used of several file structures that maintain their efficiency despite insertion and deletion of data. A B$^+$ tree index takes the form of a balanced tree in which every path from the root of the tree to a leaf of the tree is of the same length. Each node in the tree has between [n/2] and n children, where n is fixed for a particular tree.

Babbage, Charles Inventor of the analytical engine, forerunner of the computer.

Back Propagation Learning Rule Learning rule in which weights and biases are adjusted by error-derivative (delta) vectors back-propagated through the network. Back-propagation is commonly applied to feed-forward multilayer networks. Sometimes this rule is called the *generalized delta rule*.

Back Up A second, safe copy of a file, letter or data. You should do regular backups of your important work in case something goes wrong and you erase it. It might seem boring at the time, But it's far more boring to type all the information back in again. Normally you back up data on a little cassette tape or, if you don't have too much, on to floppy disks. Windows has a utility that makes backing up easy. You tell in which folder, directory or file you want to copy and whether you want to make a backup to a floppy disk or tape. Once you have made a backup, keep it well away from your main computer.

Backtracking
It is a fairly common debugging approach that can be used successfully in small programs. Beginning at the site where a symptom has been uncovered the source code is traced backward (manually) until the site of the cause is found.

Backtracking Search
Linear search routine that begins with a step multiplier of 1 and then backtracks until an acceptable reduction in performance is obtained.

Backup Copy
A copy of program and data files on a removable medium such as a floppy disk or tape, kept as protection against corruption of the original files. Keep in mind that most media degrades over time so that even through frequent recopying of programs and unchanged data isn't necessary, it's probably wise to back up the computer at least once a year.

Backup System
Computer hardware available to take over processing in the event of a failure of the primary computer systems, most common in large-scale systems such as mainframes and network.

The means recovering from a primary system failure. The systems may get simply a written procedure. The system may be simply a written procedure for reloading programs and data or it may be a program that handles the task. There are software packages that back up the entire disk, then permit incremental backup of configuration and data files(much faster than a full backup); to recover from a disk failure, the full backup is those files that are new or newer.

Bad Sector A fault in a floppy disk or hard disk. Disks are divided into tracks which contain many sectors. If you have a bad sector, it means the disk surface has been damaged at this point and that the disk drive cannot read the data there. To fix it, use the disk tools you will find in Windows or run Scandisk from the DOS prompt. For serious faults, use a special program like Norton's Disk Doctor.

Bandwidth This refers to the difference (measured in Hz), between the highest and lowest frequencies of a transmission. Most people loosely refer to bandwidth as the amount of data that can be transferred over a network connection.

Bang Metric Used to develop an indication of the size of the software to be implemented as a consequence of the analysis model.

Banker's Algorithm It needs to know the maximum number of each resource class that may be requested by each process. Using this information, a deadlock avoidance algorithm can be defined.

Barrel Shifter It also known as plus-minus-2^i (PM2I) Networks. This type of network is based on the following routing functions $B_{+I}(j) = (j+2^i)$ (Mod N), $B_{-i}(j)=(j-2^i)$(Mod N) Where $0 \le j \le N-1$, $0 \le i \le n-1$, & $n=\log_2 N$.

Basis Path Testing It is a white box testing technique first proposed by Tom McCabe. This basis path method enables the test case designer to derive a logical complexity measure of a procedural deign and sue this measure as a guide for defining a basis set of execution paths.

(1) Flow graph notation.

(2) Cyelomatic complexity

(3) Deriving test cases.

(4) Graph matrices.

At least once each statement has to be tested by following cases.

Bat Or Batch File The three-letter file name extension given to batch program files that contain batch commands stored as text. A batch file contains DOS commands that you can type at the DOS prompt, together with other control commands. It's a convenient way of grouping a series of commands you need to run frequently. To run all the commands stored in batch file, just type in the name of the file without its BAT extension and each line will be run consecutively. When you first switch on your PC a batch file called AUTOEXEC. BAT is run. This contains all the setup and configuration commands that define the environment and set up any special devices like a CD-ROM drive. To see if you have any batch files on your hard disk, use the DIR*. BAT command from the DOS prompt or the File Manager in Windows and look for.BAT file extension. To see what's inside a batch file, use the Type command in DOS.

Batch Matrix of input (or target) vectors applied to the network simultaneously. Changes to the network weights and biases are made just once for the entire set of vectors in the input matrix. (The term *batch* is being replaced by the more descriptive expression "concurrent vectors.")

Batch Processing The method of processing data in which transactions are grouped together and processed as a batch is called Batch processing.

Batching Process of presenting a set of input vectors for simultaneous calculation of a matrix of output vectors and/or new weights and biases.

Baud Rate The speed at which data is transmitted over telephone lines. For example, a 2400-baud modem sends data at a rate of 2,400 bits (about 300 characters) per second. Two modems can only connect if they can operate at the same baud rate.

Bayesian Framework Assumes that the weights and biases of the network are random variables with specified distributions.

BBS Bulletin Board System (see bulletin board).

BCD Code The term BCD stands for binary-coded decimal; it is used for decimal numbers. The decimal numbering system has ten digits, 0 to 9. Therefore, we need only four bits to represent ten digits from 0000 to 1001. The remaining numbers, 1010 (A) to 1111 (F), are considered invalid.

Behavioural Testing See Black Box Testing.

Belady's Anomaly It's a search for an optional page replacement algorithm.

Bernstein's The conditions can be used to determine how a precedence graph can be constructed for an arbitrary program.

Best First Search Tree It is known as heuristic based informed search. It always moves towards the best path and gives the best solution. The best first search algorithm retains all estimates computed for previously generated nodes and makes its selection based on the best among them all.

Place the starting node s on the queue.

If the queue is empty, return failure and stop.

If the first element on the queue is a goal node g, return success and stop, otherwise,

Remove the first element from the queue, expand it and compute the estimated goal distances for each child. Place the children on the queue (at either end) and arrange all queue elements in ascending order corresponding to goal distance from the front of the queue.

Return to step 2.

B

Beta Software An early version of a software product that is being tested and is not yet working properly. Avoid using beta software regularly, since it is not 100 percent reliable. When all the problems have been found and fixed, the software is then released. Often PC magazine's will test beta versions of a new software program to give readers an idea of what the finished version will be like when it comes out.

Beta Testing The use of a new or extensively revised computer program by a group of select user in order to unearth any buss that need to be corrected before the program is released on the open market. The developer is generally not present while testing.

Bezier Curve A geometric curve where shape is defined by two endpoints, called control handles. It's like an elastic band that you can pin down at each end and then more the middle bit around to the shape you want.

BFGS Quasi-Newton Algorithm Variation of Newton's optimization algorithm, in which an approximation of the Hessian matrix is obtained from gradients computed at each iteration of the algorithm.

Bias Neuron parameter that is summed with the neuron's weighted inputs and passed through the neuron's transfer function to generate the neuron's output.

Bias Vector Column vector of bias values for a layer of neurons.

Big Oh Notation Consider a function f(n), which is non-negative for all $n \geq 0$ such that $f(n) = O[g(n)]$ (read as "f of n equals big Oh of g on n") if and only if there exists two positive constants C and n_0 such that $|f(n)| \leq C|g(n)|$ for all $n \geq n_0$

Binary The common name for base two math's. In binary, the smallest unit is a bit (short for a binary digit). This can have one of just two values: 0 or 1. Computers count using base two, since the two values are ease to represent electrically: 0 volts for zero and (normally) 5 volts for a one.

Binary Tree A binary tree is a finite set of element that is either empty or is partitioned into three disjoint subsets.

Roots

Left sub-tree of the original tree

Right sub-tree of the original tree

BIOS Stands for Basic Input/output System, and is pronounced

Bye-oss. This is a series of instructions that manages the basic functions in your PC. For example, the BIOS look after how the keyboard works and makes sure the right character code is sent when you press a key. It also manages the disk drives and the monitor. You don't have to worry about the BIOS, and you are very unlikely to ever see it, since it's stored on a special chip inside your computer.

Bit A binary digit, the smallest unit of data used in a computer; 7 or 8 bits are typically used to represent a single character of text.

Bit Map Font A typeface of a specific size and style whose characters are made up of pixel patterns and that are available through hardware or a software program.

Bit Net A computer network devoted to academic use that provides email and file transfer services using a store and forward protocol. It is based on the IBM Network Job Entry protocols. A more recent version of Bitnet (known as Bitnet II) encapsulates the Bitnet protocol within IP packets.

B

Bitmap	Images and fonts are made up of tiny dots or pixels. If you zoom in close to a bitmap image you will see the dots grow. Compare this with a vector image, in which the shapes are described mathematically, so they appear sharp however much you zoom in.
Bits Per Second (Bps)	The speed at which bits are transmitted.
Black-Box Testing	It focuses on the functional requirements of the software. It attempts to find errors in the following categories. (1) Incorrect or Missing functions. (2) Interface Errors (3) Errors in data structures or external data base access. (4) Performance errors. (5) Initialization and termination errors. Black-box testing is sometimes called behavior testing or partition testing. Steps of testing (1) Graph-Based testing methods. (2) Equivalence partitioning. (3) Boundary value analysis. (4) Comparison testing.
BMP	The three letter file-name extension that's given to files that store bitmap image data. If you use the paint utility in Windows, you can save or open BMP files created in any other paint program.
Boc	Bell operating companies.
Boehm's Hierarchy Models	Model 1: the basic COCOMO model computers software development effort (& cost) as a function of program size expressed in estimated lines of code.

Model 2: the intermediate COCOMO model computers software development effort as a function of program size & a set of "cost drivers" that include subjective assessments of product, hardware, personnel & project attributes.

Model 3: the advanced COCOMO model incorporates all characteristics of the intermediate version with an assessment of the cost driver's impact on each step (analysis, design, etc.) of the software engineering process.

Booch Method It encompasses both a "micro development process" & a "macro development process".

Boot Disk Disk containing the operating system that is loaded when a PC is switched on, the boot up instructions tell the hardware to read in the operating system software.

Normally, the boot disk is your main hard disk. But you can use a floppy disk as a boot disk, if it is formatted as a system or boot disk.

Boot, Boot Up To start up a computer. This is process carried out when your PC is switched on. First, a sequence of instructions stored with the BIOS in a chip is executed and they tell the computer to look on the boot disk for the main operating system. The PC tests the floppy drive A: and then the hard drive C: for a valid boot disk that contains the operating system.

Bootstrap Compiler A compiler is a complex enough program that we would like to write it in a friendlier language than assembly language. In the UNIX programming environment, compilers are usually written in C. even C compliers are written in C. using the facilities offered by a language to compile itself is the essence of bootstrapping. For bootstrapping, a compiler is characterized by 3 languages : the source language 'S' that compiles the target language 'T' that generates code for and the implementation language 'I' that it is written in.

Bounce If you send email and it fails to arrive at its intended receipt for any reason (incorrect user name, network failure, etc.), the message "bounces" and returns to you. The subject line in a bounced message usually says something like: Undeliverable mail or Message undeliverable.

Boyce-Codd Normal Form A relation R is said to be in BCNF if it is in 3NF and every determinant is a candidate key.

Branch – And-Bound Search This strategy applies to problems having a graph search space where more than one alternative path may exist between two nodes. This strategy saves all path length (or costs) from a node to all generated nodes and chooses the shortest path for further expansion. It then compares the new, path lengths with all old ones and again chooses the shortest path for expansion. In this way, any path to a goal node is certain to be a minimal length path.

Break A signal sentence from a user's terminal to the network, which causes interruption of an activity.

Brent's Search Linear search that is a hybrid of the golden section search and a quadratic interpolation.

Bresenham's Line Algorithm An accurate and efficient raster line – generating algorithm.

Bridge It is operated on the data link layer and is not require checking upper layer information. A bridge eliminates unnecessary traffic and minimizes the chances of collisions occurring on a network by dividing the segments and filtering traffic based on MAC address. Bridge filters network traffic by only looking at the MAC address.

Broadband Coaxial Cable It is used for analog transmission on standard cable television cabling. Broadband cables can be used up to 450 MHz and can run for nearly 100 km due to the analog signaling, which is much less critical than digital signaling.

Broadcast Networks It has a single communication channel that is shared by all the machines on the network. Broadcast systems generally allow the possibility of addressing a packet to all destinations by using a special code in the address field. When a packet with this code is transmitted, it is received & processed by every machine on the network. This mode of operation is called broadcasting. Some broadcast systems also support transmission to a subset of the machines, something known as multicasting.

Browsers It is software, which allows us to easily display web pages and navigate the web. There are many flavors of web browsers but they can be grouped into two basic categories. They are

1. Text-only: A text-only browser such as Lynx allows you to visit web pages without showing art or page structure.

2.Graphical: to display the complete web page along with multimedia, a graphical browser such as Netscape Navigator or Internet Explorer is used.

Browsing To move through a multimedia program or through a list of files in no particular order. You control which page you go to next and what you view.

Bubble Sort	**Bubble sort**, sometimes incorrectly referred to as **sinking sort**, is a simple sorting algorithm that works by repeatedly stepping through the list to be sorted, comparing each pair of adjacent items and swapping them if they are in the wrong order. The pass through the list is repeated until no swaps are needed, which indicates that the list is sorted. The algorithm gets its name from the way smaller elements "bubble" to the top of the list. Because it only uses comparisons to operate on elements, it is a comparison sort. Although the algorithm is simple, most of the other sorting algorithms are more efficient for large lists.
Buddy Memory Allocation	The **buddy memory allocation** technique is a memory allocation algorithm that divides memory into partitions to try to satisfy a memory request as suitably as possible. This system makes use of splitting memory into halves to try to give a best-fit.
Buddy System	The **buddy system** is a procedure in which two people, the "buddies", operate together as a single unit so that they are able to monitor and help each other.
Buffer	It is the part of main memory available for storage of copies of disk blocks.
Buffer Manager	The subsystem responsible for the allocation of Buffer space.
Buffering	Another solution to the slowness of input/ output devices. It attempts to keep the CPU & the input/ output devices busy all the time.
Bug	An error in a program that means it does not work properly. (See also Beta), See the term fault.

Bullet A symbol – often a filled circle or square- printed in front of a line of text to draw attention to it. If you are using a Windows word processor, you can add bullet by changing the font to symbol or windings.

Bulletin Board Service (Bbs) Computer you can call up and connect to via a modem and a phone line. Bulletin boards normally have lots of free software that you can download, together with areas called forums where you can discuss topics with other users. More sophisticated systems have links to other bulletin computers or even the Internet. When you sign up with a BBS you are given an account which has your own user name and password. To use it again, you need to enter your user name and password. To access a bulletin board you need to have a modem. You also need communications software. All versions of windows come with free communications software to get you started.

Byte A group of eight bits – that's eight binary digits-which is the usual form in which data is manipulated within a computer. One byte can hold numbers between 0 and 255.for example, each different letter of the alphabet, numeral and punctuation mark has a special code that describes it (see ASCII) code. This code is stored within one byte, and so your computer can identify 256 different characters.

C

Cable A set of wires connecting pieces of computer hardware.

Cache, Cache Memory A section of very high-speed memory that is used to temporarily store data before it is used by the PC's processor. A cache can dramatically speed up the effective rate at which data is read from a hard disk drive. The computer reads more than is requested and stores the excess into read data. The memory used for the cache can be up to 100,000 times faster than a hard disk drive.

CAD/CAM Stands for Computer Aided-Design. It is special software that allows designers and architects to draw precise blue prints on screen, and then model them in 3D to see how the design will appear in real life before a product is manufactured or a building erected.

Caddy A flat plastic container used to hold a CD, inserted into a CD-ROM drive.

CAL Computer Augmented Learning. The reinforcement of learning with the use of the computer.

Calculator A software utility that's supplied with Windows and works just like a normal calculator. To start the calculator, choose Start/Programs/Accessories in windows.

Calendar A simple calendar and diary supplied with windows.

Calibrate To adjust a monitor or joystick so that it is responding correctly and accurately to the signals or movements. For example, this ensures that the monitor is displaying a true representation of the color that will be printed.

Candidate Keys All attribute combinations inside a relation that can serve as primary key are candidate keys as they are candidate for the primary key position. In such a case, we must decide which of the candidate keys will be used as primary key and remaining would be considered as alternate key.

Carriage Return The <ENTER> or <RETURN> key on your keyboard. On-line commands often must be followed by <CR>.

Cascade-Forward Network Layered network in which each layer only receives inputs from previous layers.

Cascading Style Sheets Style sheets are powerful mechanism for adding styles (e.g., fonts, colors, spacing) to web documents. They enforce standards and uniformity throughout a website and provide numerous attributes to create dynamic effects with style sheets, text and image formatting properties can be predefining in a single list. HTML elements as a web page can then be bound to the style sheet.

Cascading Windows A way of arranging lots of windows on screen so that they overlap, with only the title bar and caption showing. This is a neat and efficient way of displaying lots of windows at once. An alternative is to tile the windows. Each is displayed beside the next with no overlap. Another alternative is to reduce each window to an icon, or, in O.S Windows, on to the status bar at the bottom of the screen.

CC (Carbon Copy) The prompt in an e-mail program which allows the user to enter one or more ID's to send copies of a message.

C

CD Stands for Compact Disc. A small plastic disc that is used to store up to 650Mb or 700Mb of data. The data is stored in the form of tiny holes etched on to the surface of the disc. A CD drive spins disc and uses a laser beam to read the holes in the surface. A CD can store any type of computer data from images to text to music. However it can only be read by a user. You cannot save data on to a CD. A CD normally refers to a normal music disc which can be played in your hi-fi or in your PC's CD player. You just plug in a pair of headphones and use the media player utility to start playing. In the computer world, the same type of plastic disc is used to store files and data and is called a CD-ROM (Read Only Memory).

CD-Audio Or CD-DA Stands for Compact Disc-Digital Audio. Standard that defines how music can be stored as a series of numbers (digital form) on a CD.

CD-i Compact Disc for audio and visual for movies, reference, training courses and video games. It can be interactive but is not programmable; it is viewed through a television and CD-I player, not a computer.

CDPD Cellular digital packet data. It also known as direct digital cellular service.

CD-Rom Drive A computer accessory used to access CD-ROM discs. Internal CD-ROM drives are installed inside the computer system. External versions have their own enclosure and power supply and are connected to the computer by a cable. Many computers now include a built-in CD-ROM drive as standard equipment.

Cell — An area in computer memory that holds a unit of information, such as a character.

A basic unit of data in a spreadsheet.

Cellular Multi-Lists File Organization — A further modification of the multi-list is inspired by the fact that many storage media are divided into pages, which can be retrieved one at a time. A K-list may cross several page boundaries which mean that several pages may have to be accessed to retrieve one record. A modified multi-list structure which avoids this is called a cellular multi-list. The K-lists are limited so that they will not cross the page (cell) boundaries.

CFG — File name extension for a configuration file.

CGM (Computer Graphics Metafile) — A file name extension for a vector image, a type of graphics file.

Channel Allocation Methods & System For A Common Channel

Method	Description
FDM	➔ Dedicate a frequency band to each station.
TDM	➔ Dedicate a time slot to each station.
Pure ALOHA	➔ Unsynchronized transmission at any instant.
Slotted ALOHA	➔ Random transmission in well-defined time slots.
1-persistent CSMA	➔ Standard carries sense multiple access.
Nonpersistent CSMA	➔ Random delay when channel is sensed busy.
P-Persistent CSMA	➔ CSMA, but with a probability of p of persisting.
CSMA/CD	➔ CSMA, but abort on detecting a collision.
Bit map	➔ Round robin scheduling using a bit map.

Binary countdown → highest numbered ready station goes next.

Tree walks → Reduced contention by selective enabling.

Wavelength division→ a dynamic FDM scheme for fiber.

MACA, MACAW → Wireless LAN protocols.

GSM → FDM plus TDM for cellular radio.

CDPD → Packet radio within an AMPS channel.

CDMA→ Everybody speaks at once but in a different language.

Ethernet→ CSMA/CD with binary exponential back off.

Token bus → Logical ring on a physical bus.

Token rings → Capture the token to send a frame.

DQDB → Distributed Queuing on a two-bus MAN.

FDDI → Fiber-optic token ring.

HIPPI → Crossbar using 50-100 twisted pairs.

Fiber channel → Crossbar using fiber optics.

SPADE → EDM with dynamic channel allocation.

ACTS → TDM with centralized slot allocation.

Binder → TDM with ALOHA when slot owner is not interested.

Crowther→ ALOHA with slot owner getting to keep it.

Roberts → channel time reserved in advance by ALOHA.

Chap (Challenge-Handshake Authentication Protocol) An authentication method that can be used when connecting to an Internet Service Provider. CHAP allows Service Provider. CHAP allows you to login to your provider automatically, without the need for a terminal screen. It is more secure than the Password Authentication Protocol (another widely used authentication method) since it does not send passwords in text format.

Character A letter or number that is displayed or printed. The shape of each character is determined by the typeface and font that's used. Each font includes 256 different characters, normally with a-z and A-Z together with foreign characters, symbols and punctuation marks.

Character Map A utility that is provided with any O.S to allow you access to all 256 characters that make up a font rather than the limited range you can access from the keyboard. The extra characters include foreign characters and symbols.

Charalambous' Search Hybrid line search that uses a cubic interpolation together with a type of sectioning.

Chat Another term for IRC. Also, an acronym meaning Conversational Hypertext Access Technology.

Chip Small electronic device at the heart of every PC. A chip is a small thin piece of silicon crystal on to which is etched a tiny circuits' with hundreds of components. These components will do simple mathematical operations such as adding and subtracting numbers (in a memory chip). If ever you open your PC you'll see a mass of small black boxes with tens of metal legs on each side, they are the chips.

C

Chomsky Normal Form One kind of normal form we can look for is one in which the number of symbols on the right of a production are strictly limited. In particular, we can ask that the string on the right of a production consists of no more than two symbols, one instance of this the Chomsky normal form.

Class A 'Class' embodies the concepts of an abstract data type by defining both the set of values of a given type and set of operations that can be performed on those values.

Object-Oriented programming constructs modeled out of data types called classes. A class encloses both data and functions that operate on the data.

Class A class is a collection of objects that share common properties and relationships.

Classification Association of an input vector with a particular target vector.

Clean Room Software Engineering It is a formal approach to software development that can lead to software that has remarkably high quality. It uses box structure specification (formal specification) for analysis and design modeling and emphasizes correctness, verification, rather than testing, as the primary mechanism for finding and removing errors, statistical use testing is applied to develop the failure rate information necessary to certify the reliability of delivered software.

The clean room approach begins with analysis and design models that use a box structure representation. A "box" encapsulates the system at a specific level of abstraction.

Client In Internet terms, it's an application that performs a specific function, such as Telnet or FTP. It's the front-end to an Internet process. In more general terms, a client is computer system or processes that request a service of another computer system or process. The much talked about client-server architecture refers to a workstation requesting the contents of a file from a server.

Clip Art A library of drawings or photographs that you can use in your presentations, reports or desktop publishing documents. Normally, there are no copyright fees if you use the images for non-commercial use, you'll find that most presentation programs, like Harvard Graphics or Microsoft Power point, come with hundreds of pre-drawn images, borders and icons in a clip art library.

Clock A tiny crystal in your computer that sends out a regular signal hundreds of thousands of times every second. It's used by all electronic components to keep in time with each other so that data is not lost when it's transferred. The central processing unit normally carries out instruction every clock pulse, so the faster the clock, the more the instructions it carries out. The speed of a processor, and so the clock, is measured in Megahertz (MHz) or Gigahertz (GHz), which represent one million or billion pulses every second. Example, if processor that runs at 50MHz uses a clock that sends 50 million signals every second.

Cluster The smallest elements that the DOS operating system software that controls your PC can read from or write to a disk.

Cluster Testing — It is one step in the integration testing of object Oriented software. Here, a cluster of collaborating classes is exercised by designing test cases that attempt to uncover errors in the collaborations.

Clustering File Organization — In this organization, records of several different relations can be stored in the same file. Related records of the different relations are stored on the same block, so that one i/o operation fetches related records from all the relations.

CMOS Logic — A complementary MOSFET (CMOS) is obtained by connecting a p-channel and n-channel MOSFET in series, with drains tied together and the output is taken the common drain. Input is applied at the common gate formed by connecting the two gates together. In a CMOS, p-channel and n-channel enhancement MOS devices are fabricated on the same chip, which makes its fabrication more complicated and reduces the pacing density. But because of negligibly small power consumption, CMOS is ideally suited for battery-operated systems.

CMY Color Model — A color model defined with the primary colors cyan, magenta & yellow (CMY) is useful for describing color output to hard copy devices.

CMYK — Stands for Cyan, Magenta, Yellow and black. A method of describing any color by the percentages of these colors. Normally used in a high-end graphics programs.

Coaxial Cable — A cable made up of an outer metal tubular conductor surrounding an insulated inner conducting core, used for high-frequency transmission such as for telephone or television.

COBOL (Common Business Oriented Language) A structured computer programming language for business application that uses a vocabulary of familiar English words and phrases.

COCOMO : Constructive Cost Model (1) Organic mode: relatively small, simple software projects in which small teams with good application experience work to a set of less than rigid requirements.

(2) Semi-detached mode: an intermediate (in size and complexity) software project in which teams with mixed experience levels must meet a mix of rigid and less than rigid requirements.

(3) Embedded mode: a software project that must be developed within a set of tight hardware, software & operational constraints.

Code Generation The final phase of the compiler is the code generator. The code generator takes an input as intermediate representation of the source program and produces as output an equivalent target program.

Code Optimization It attempts to improve the intermediate code, so that faster running machine code will results. The code optimization may incorporate both machine dependent and machine independent techniques.

Cohesion It is a natural extension of the information hiding concept. It performs the following tasks

(1) Computer supplementary data based on original computed data.

(2) Produces a report (with graphical content) on the user's workstation.

(3) Performs follow-up calculations requested by the user.

(4) Updates a data base.

(5) Enables menu selection for subsequent processing.

C

Cold Boot Restarting a computer that is completely shut down.

Collate To print multiple copies of a document in a correct order. If you want three copies of a document, instead of the usual method of printing three copies of page and so on, the word processing software is clever to print all the pages in order and repeat this three times.

Color Crt In graphics systems are designed as RGB monitors. An RGB color system with 24 bits of storage per pixel is generally referred to as a full-color system or a true-color system.

Color Depth The number of different colors that can be displayed by any single pixel in a display. Determined by the number of color bits in each pixel.

Color Palette The selection of colors that is currently being used in an image. Even though a pixel might have only eight color bits, and so can display 256 different colors, you can choose these 256 colors from a range of millions of different colors: your choice of colors is the color palette.

Com The file name extension for a command file, program file that is activated when the file name is brought to the command line by user or another program.

Combinational Circuits It is interconnected circuits of gates according to certain rule to produce an output depending on its input value.

Command An instruction you give to an on-line network to carry out a specific action.

Common Process Framework Defines an organization's approach to software development and maintenance. It identifies the software engineering paradigm that is applied to build & maintenance software, the tasks, milestone & deliverables that will be required.

Communication Commonality The degree to which standard interfaces, protocols, and bandwidth are used.

Compact Disk A digital disk form which data is read by a special laser. The laser reads binary data as 0's and 1's by distinguishing between microscopic flat and pitted dots on the surface of the disk.

Compaction See in relocation.

Competitive Learning Unsupervised training of a competitive layer with the instars rule or Kohonen rule. Individual neurons learn to become feature detectors. After training, the layer categorizes input vectors among its neurons.

Competitive Transfer Function Accepts a net input vector for a layer and returns neuron outputs of 0 for all neurons except for the winner, the neuron associated with the most positive element of the net input n.

Competitive Layer Layer of neurons in which only the neuron with maximum net input has an output of 1 and all other neurons have an output of 0. Neurons compete with each other for the right to respond to a given input vector.

Completeness The degree to which implementation of required function has been achieved.

Compression To reduce the size of a file by encoding the data. For example, if the file contains five letters as next to each other, which takes five bytes of space, the compression software could encode this to 5A which takes two bytes of space. The compression uses all sorts of encoding tricks to code the way data is stored to reduce the space it takes. Software is normally used to compress a file or all the data on a disk drive, but don't forget that decompression software is needed when you want to read the data again.

C

Computer "Computer" is a LATIN word, which means to "Calculate". There are 3 types of computers. 1. Analog computer 2.Digital computer 3.Hybrid computer.

Factors	Analog computer	Digital computer
1) Input	Physical variables	Alphanumeric
2) Output	Graphical	Numeric & graphical
3) Processing (Operations)	Integration	Arithmetic & logical
4) Set up	As the problem changes new set up is made	The H/W need not be changed with the problem.
5) Memory unit	Normally not required	Necessary to store data & instructions.
6) Accuracy	Limited	High degree of accuracy.
7) Processor	OPAMP	Microprocessor
8)Application	Simulating physical system by mathematical analogy	Useful in solving both scientific & business problems.

Computer Animation The creation of moving images especially of cartoons or special effect with the aid of a computer, as for television or motion pictures.

Computer Science The study of theories and methods involved in development of computer systems, hardware, and software.

Computer Security The process of protecting a computer, computer network, or computer programs and data form access by unauthorized persons.

Computer Software It is information transformer-producing, managing, acquiring, modifying, displaying or transmitting information that can be as simple as a single bit or as Complex as a multimedia simulation.

Conciseness The compactness of the program in terms of liner of code.

Concrete Class It is a class that is instantiable; that is, it can have direct instances. A concrete class may have abstract subclasses (but they in turn must have concrete descendants).

Concurrent Input Vectors Name given to a matrix of input vectors that are to be presented to a network simultaneously. All the vectors in the matrix are used in making just one set of changes in the weights and biases.

Condition Testing It is a test case design method that exercises' the logical conditions contained in a program module. A simple condition is a Boolean variable or a relational expression. Its advantages are

1. Measurement of test coverage of a condition is simple

2. The test coverage of conditions is a program provides guidance for the generation of additional tests for the program.

Conference An electronic meeting place dedicated to a particular subject where users come to participate in discussions or group projects. Conferences can be used to post a variety of information such as news services, newsletters, and statistics; also called "newsgroups", "bulletin boards", or "Echoes". And electronic conference provides a many-to-many communication medium, as opposed to the person-to-person nature of e-mail. All conferences have a particular subject or purpose, and the topics and responses they contain might provide items of news, ideas, restricted access, allowing some users to write messages, some only to read, and some neither. The person responsible for the technical maintenance and /or community communication is called the "Conference facilitator".

Confidence The probability that the result returned by the speech engine matches what a speaker said. Speech engines generally return confidence scores that reflect the probability; the higher the score, the more likely the engine's result is correct.

Configure To set the function of software or hardware to your

particular setting. You can configure windows so that it displays a different color background, of so ha it uses a larger font that's easier to read. If you install a new software application there are two main steps; the first is the installation, which simply creates a new folder and copies the files on to your hard disk from the floppy disk or CD-ROM. Once the program is installed, you can configure it to work the way it looks and works. The Tools/ Customize option lets you change the icons and menus that are displayed, while the Tools/Customize option lets you change the initial settings for the software.

Conjugate Gradient Algorithm In the conjugate gradient algorithms, a search is performed along conjugate directions, which produces generally faster convergence than a search along the steepest descent directions.

Connection One-way link between neurons in a network.

Connection Strength Strength of a link between two neurons in a network. The strength, often called weight, determines the effect that one neuron has on another.

Consistency The use of uniform design & documentation techniques

throughout the software development project.

Context-Free Grammar The productions in a regular grammar are restricted in two ways: the left side must be a single variable, while the right side has a special form. To create grammars that are more powerful, we must relax some of these restrictions. By retaining the restriction on the left side, but permitting anything on the right, we get context-free grammar.

Continuous Speech System A continuous speech system operates on speech in which words are connected together, i.e. not separated by pauses. Continuous speech is more difficult to handle because of a variety of effects. First, it is difficult to find the start and end points of words. Another problem is "co-articulation". The production of each phoneme is affected by the production of surrounding phonemes, and similarly the start and end of words are affected by the preceding and following words. The recognition of continuous speech is also affected by the rate of speech (fast speech tends to be harder).

Control Key: (Ctrl) This is a key on the keyboard (in the bottom right and left corners of the main character pad) that is used for special functions. The control key is used with another key. You press and hold down the control key and then press a second key and you will activate a special function. The keys and their functions all depend on the way the software was written.

In many windows-based applications there is a set of standard control key functions. Ctrl–S will usually save the current document, Ctrl-N will create new document, and Ctrl-P will print the document out. To move around any windows application, Ctrl-right-arrow will move the cursor one word to the right and Ctrl-left-arrow will one word to the left. Ctrl-up-arrow will move you to the beginning of the paragraph and Ctrl-down-arrow will move to the you to the end of the document.

Control Panel This is a collection of icons that allow you to configure the basic functions of windows and your PC. Within the Control Panel here are icons to define the fonts that are installed on your computer, the color of the background to Windows, the type of printer that's installed, how a network works, Add or Remove Programs as well as a mass of other options.

Control Structure Testing Although basis path testing is simple & highly effective, it is not sufficient in itself. So other variations on control structure testing has been made:

(1) Condition testing.

(2) Dataflow testing.

(3) Loop testing.

Controlled Centralized(Cc) See in software team.

Controlled Decentralized (Cd) See in software team.

Cood & Yourdon Method It is often viewed as one of the easiest object oriented analysis (OOA) methods to learn. Modeling notation is relatively simple & guidelines for developing the analysis model are straight forward.

Cordless Telephones It started as a way to allow people to walk around the house while on the phone. The First generation of cordless Telephones, known as CT-1 in U.S & CEPT-1 in Europe. Range is typically 100 to 300 meters.

Correctness The extent to which a program satisfies its specification and fulfills the customer's mission objectives.

Counters It is a sequential circuit. A counter is register whose value is incriminated by 1 on the occurrence of some event. When the value stored in counter reaches the maximum value it can store, the next incremented value becomes zero. The counters are used for counting the number of times of an event occurs and are useful for generating the timing signals for controlling the sequence of operations in digital computers. There are two types of counters asynchronous and synchronous. In asynchronous counter the state of one flip-flop changes at a time while in synchronous counter the state of all the flip-flop can be changed at the same time.

Coupling It is a measure of interconnection among modules in a structure. Compiling depends on the interface complexity between modules, the point at which entry or reference is made to a module, and what data pass across the interface.

Courseware Educational programs designed for in-school use.

Cpu Or Central Processing Unit The main processor chip in a computer which responds to software instructions and controls peripherals and memory.

Cpu Scheduling CPU scheduling deals with the problem of deciding which of the processes in the ready queue is to be allocated the CPU.

There are many different CPU scheduling algorithms.

Performance criteria.

First come first served.

Shortest-job-first.

Priority.

Preemptive algorithms.

Round Robin.

Multi-level-queues.

Multi-level feedback queues.

Highest-Priority First.

Longest-Job-First.

Last-Come-First Served.

Cracker Substantially different from hackers, crackers are users who try to gain illegal access to computers. They are usually malicious in their intentions.

Crammer's Rule A simple method of solving simultaneous linear equations by determinants.

Credit Cards These cards are issued by the finance institutions which gives liberty to purchase desired products on credit. Payment of the products is made by the credit card companies on behalf of the credit holders. In turn these companies forward bills to the costumers. In order to purchase a product or a service, the credit card holders send their credit card details to the service providers and credit card organization will carry out the remaining functions like other cash transaction.

Critical Path Method (CPM) The **critical path method (CPM)** is an algorithm for scheduling a set of project activities. It is an important tool for effective project management. The essential technique for using CPM is to construct a model of the project that includes the following:

A list of all activities required to complete the project (typically categorized within a work breakdown structure),

The time (duration) that each activity will take to complete,

The dependencies between the activities and,

Logical end points such as milestones or deliverable items.

CRT Cathode-Ray tube. The operation of most video monitors is based on the standard CRT design, but several other technologies exist & solid-state monitors may eventually predominate.

Cursor A highlighted or blinking block, line or underscore on a computer monitor that indicates where you are currently typing.

Cyberspace The world of computers and the society that gathers around them, as referred to by William Gibson in his fantasy novel Neuromancer. It now loosely refers to the online world and even more loosely to the Internet.

Cycle Single presentation of an input vector, calculation of output, and new weights and biases.

Cyclomatic Complexity It is software metric that provides a quantitative measure of the logical complexity of a program. It defines the number of independent paths in the basis set of a program and provides us with an upper bound for the number of tests that must be conducted to ensure that all statements have been executed at least once.

C

Cyclomatic Complexity (Or Conditional Complexity)

It is software metric (measurement). It was developed by Thomas J. McCabe in 1976 and is used to indicate the complexity of a program. It is a quantitative measure of logical strength of the program. It directly measures the number of linearly independent paths through a program's source code. The concept, although not the method, is somewhat similar to that of general text complexity measured by the Flesch-Kincaid Readability Test. Cyclomatic complexity is computed using the control flow graph of the program: the nodes of the graph correspond to indivisible groups of commands of a program, and a directed edge connects two nodes if the second command might be executed immediately after the first command. Cyclomatic complexity may also be applied to individual functions, modules, methods or classes within a program.

Mathematically, the cyclomatic *complexity* of a structured program is defined with reference to the control flow graph of the program, a directed graph containing the basic blocks of the program, with an edge between two basic blocks if control may pass from the first to the second. The complexity **M** is then defined as $M = E - N + 2P$,

Where E = the number of edges of the graph, N = the number of nodes of the graph, P = the number of connected components (exit nodes).

D

DAT File name extension for a configuration file.

Data Any collection of numbers, characters or symbols, which are used by a computer. Once a computer has finished processing all the data, it then presents this as information, which can be understood by a user.

Data Abstraction It refers to the act of representing essential features without including the background details or explanations. In other words, when the data is not accessible to the outside world and only those functions which contain in that class can access it.

Data Archives Data used in operational data processing is normally stored in many organizations as back up or for legal reasons. These are called data archives.

Data Cleansing Bcforc data enters the data warehouse, the extraction, transformation and cleaning (ETL) process ensures that the data passes the data quality threshold.

Data Commonality The use of standard data structures and types throughout the program.

Data Definition Language (Ddl) A database schema is specified by a set of definitions

expressed by a special language.

Data Dictionary In database management systems, a file that defines the basic organization of a database. A data dictionary contains a list of all files in the database, the number of records in each file, and the names and types of each field. Most database management systems keep the data dictionary hidden from users to prevent them from accidentally destroying its contents.

Data dictionaries do not contain any actual data from the database, only book-keeping information for managing it. Without a data dictionary, however, a database management system cannot access data from the database.

Data Directory It is a file that contains metadata – that is, data about data. This file is consulted before actual data are read or modified in the database system.

Data Encryption Key (Dek) Much like an actual key used for locking and reopening

doors, desk are used for the encryption and decoding of

message text, sometimes in the form of a digital signature.

Data Flow Diagram (Dfd) It's used for two purposes

1. To provide an indication of how data are transformed as they move through the system.

2. To depict the functions (and sub functions) that transform the data flow.

Data Fragmentation A distributed system supports data fragmentation if a given relation can be divided up into pieces or fragments for physical storage purposes. Data may be fragmented in one of following ways: Horizontal Fragmentation, Vertical Fragmentation or Mixed Fragmentation.

Data Glove Used to grasp a "virtual" object. The glove is constructed with a series of sensors that detect hand & finger motions. A 2-D projection of the scene can be viewed on a video monitor, or 3-D projection can be viewed with a headset.

Data Independence The ability to modify a schema definition in one level without affecting a schema definition in the next higher level is called data independence. There are two levels

1. Physical data independence

2. Logical data independence.

Data Log — It is a nonprocedural query language that is based on the logic programming language prolog.

Data Manipulation Language (DML) — It is a language that enables users to access or manipulate data as organized by the appropriate data model.

Data Mining — It refers loosely to finding relevant information, or "discovering knowledge", from a large volume of data. Like knowledge discovery in artificial intelligence, data mining attempts to discover statistical rules & patterns automatically from data.

Data Mining — It is the discovery of useful patterns in data. Data mining are used for prediction analysis and classification. E.g., what is the likelihood that a customer will migrate to a competitor?

Data Mining — The archived data may be analyzed to obtain tactical and strategic information. This is called data mining.

Data Modeling — data modeling answers specific questions that are relevant to any data processing application. What are the primary data objects to be processed by the system? What is the composition of each data object and what attributes describe the object? Where do the object currently reside? What are the relationships between objects? What is the relationship between the objects and the processes that transform them?

To answer these questions, data modeling methods make use of the entity relationship diagram (ERD).

D

Data Models	A collection of conceptual tools for describing data, data relationships, data semantics and consistency constraints.
Data Replication	It means storing some data at more than one site. In a distributed database data may be replicated in any of the following ways: No replication: In this scheme, the database is fragmented and a fragment stored at a site is not stored anywhere else i.e., a fragment remains with one single site. Partial Replication: In this scheme, some fragments (not all) are stored at multiple sites. The number of copies of each fragment can range from one up to the total number of sites in the distributed system. Full Replication: In this scheme, the whole database is replicated at every site in the distributed system. It improves availability and performance but slows down the system.
Data Repositories	The data warehouse repository is the database that stores active data of business value for an organization. The data warehouse modeling design is optimized for data analysis.
Data Time	Your PC has a tiny battery inside it that allows one area of memory to permanently store the current time and date. If you need to change this, use the control panel.
Data Visualization Tools	It is used to display data from the data repository. Often data visualization is combined with data mining and OLAP tools. It can allow the user to manipulate data to show relevancy and patterns.

be retrieved. The same method used to encode is usually just reversed in order to decode. It is a combinational circuit that converts binary information from n input lines to a maximum of 2^n unique output lines.

Dedicated Line A communications line that is used solely for computer connections. If you buy an additional phone line for your modem, that's a dedicated line. There are other types of dedicated lines (such as T3s and T1s) that are used for larger network entities.

Default The options that are used if no others are specified. For example, if you run a word processor and start typing a letter, it will use the default typeface and the default paper size and margins. You can always change these settings later.

Defragmentation When a file is saved to disk the operating system does not necessarily save it over a continuous area. If the disk is full, it might have to split the file and save it in chunks in different places. This doesn't matter to the software or the user, but it does not make it slower to retrieve the file. If you think your hard disk is slower than it used to be a few months ago, you could well be right. The answer is to use the defragmentation utility that will reorganize your hard disk so that all the files are stored in continuous areas.

Delete Key To select text or other data and remove it from a file; to remove a file from your disk. If you delete a section of text, you can immediately undelete (using the Edit/Undelete) function. If you delete a file from your disk, you can sometime undelete it depending on your PC's setup. If you are running Windows, there is a recycle Bin that stores files that have deleted for a period of time – double click on the bin icon to see your file.

D

Deletion Time The time takes to delete a data item. This includes the time it takes to find the item to be deleted as well as the time it takes to update the index structure.

Delta Rule See Widrow-Hoff learning rule.

Delta Vector The delta vector for a layer is the derivative of a network's output error with respect to that layer's net input vector.

Demand Paging Similar to a paging system with swapping[see lazy swapping]

Democratic Decentralized (DD) See the software Team.

Dense Index An index record appears for every search key value in the file. The record contains the search key value and a pointer to the record.

Depth First Search Depth first search are performed by dividing downward into a tree as quickly as possible. It does this by always generating a child node from the most recently expanded node, then generating that child's children, and so on until a goal is found or some cutoff depth point d is reached. If a goal is not found when a leaf node is reached or at the cutoff point, the program back track's to the most recently expanded node and generates another of its children. This process continues until a goal is found or failure occurs.

Depth First Search Algorithm Place the starting node s on the queue

If the queue is empty, return failure and stop.

If the first element on the queue is a goal node t, return success and stop. Otherwise,

Remove and expand the first element, & place the children at the front of the queue (in any order).

Return to step 2.

Design It is the first step in the development phase for any engineered product or system. Defined as "the process of applying various techniques and principles for the purpose of defining a device, a process or a system in sufficient detail to permit its physical realization.

Desktop In Windows, Desktop is the term that defines what you see on your screen when Windows first start up. The icons, status bar, start button and the Recycle Bin are all sitting together on the Desktop. It's a rather odd concept to grasp at first, but it is probably easiest to imagine as if it were a real desk. On your desk you have folders, some open (the icons and windows), a waste bin, and a small filing cabinet (OK, it's quite a big desk!), which is the My Computer icon. The Desktop contains all these icons and objects, together with a background pattern and any windows or applications that might be open.

Desktop Computer A personal or micro or mini-computer small enough to fit on a desk but too large to be easily portable.

Desktop Icons Icons that are displayed on the Desktop. There are two icons that are always on your Windows Desktop: My Computer and Recycle Bin. If you are connected to a network, you might also see an Inbox icon, which lets you send and receive messages. Any other icons are called shortcuts and provide a link to a program or to a document. You can create a shortcut to any file by highlighting the file in Explorer and clicking on the right mouse button. You'll see a menu option that says create shortcut. For example, if you create a shortcut to a document file called Letter to Boss; this will appear on your Desktop. If you double-click on this icon Windows will start your word processor and automatically load the document.

Desktop Publishing (DTP) The design, layout and printing if documents, books and magazines using special desktop publishing software.

Desktop publishing software allows you to define the size and shape of a page, position blocks of text and pictures and manipulate the text to change its size, color, typeface, leading and alignment. The use of a computer for setting type, creating graphics effects and laying out pages for reproduction.

Device Directors The particular information kept for each file in the directory Varies from O.S to O.S the following is a list of some of the information which may be kept in a directory entry. Not all systems keep all this information, of course.

(a) File name

(b) File type

(c) Location

(d) Size

(e) Current position

(f) Protection

(g) Usage count

(h) Time, date & process identification.

Device Independence The ability to run a program with different input/output Devices.

DFD A deterministic finite accepter is defined by the quintuple, M=(Q, Σ, S_0, q_0, F)where Q is a finite set of internal states, Σ is a finite set of symbols called the input alphabet, S_0 :Q * Σ → Q is a total function called the transition function, q_o → Q is the initial state, F → Q is a set of final states.

DHTML (Dynamic Hypertext Markup Language)	It is a technology which combines HTML with cascading style sheets (CSS) and scripting languages. HTML specifies web pages elements like table, frame, paragraph, bullet list etc. Cascading style sheets can be used to determine an elements size, color, position and a number of other features.
Dialup	A widely used method of accessing the internet. A dialup connection uses regular phone lines to connect one computer to another via modem.
Dictation Software	A type of computer application that allows users to speak freely as the application transcribes each word the users say. This kind of software is almost always Speaker dependent.
Dictionary	A large set of data used by a speech engine while doing speech recognition that defines the phonemes in a language or dialect.
Digital	Used in computerize to describe information that can be represented by a collection of bits.
Digital Cameras	Cameras that do not use photographic film. The light images are converted into computer data by special electronics and are stored in memory chips within the cameras. The images can be transferred to computers and used by application programs, such as web editors and browsers.
Digitalizes	A common device for drawing, painting, or interactively selecting coordinate positions on an object is a digitizer.
DIR	A DOS command that displays the files stored in the current directory.
Directed Dialogue	An approach to speech application design that prompts users to say specific phrases. Contrast with natural language.

D

Directory In DOS, a way of organizing files on a disk. A directory can contain files or other sub-directories. A good way of thinking of directories is to imagine a filling cabinet: the cabinet is the disk. Each drawer a directory. If you open a directory, you'll see lots of folders which are sub-directories. Look in a folder and you will see documents or files.

Dirty Bit Each page or frame may have a dirty bit associated with it in the Hardware. The dirty bit for a page is set by the Hardware whenever any word or byte in the page is written into, indicating when the page has been modified. Overhead can be reduced by the using a dirty bit.

Disk A flat, circular piece of plastic that's coated with a substance that is capable of being magnetized and so store information. A hard disk contains of several rigid plastic disks arranged in parallel; a floppy disk has one thing; flexible plastic disk. The disk spins at high speed and data is written to or read from the surface of the disk by a magnetic head much like the one in a cassette recorder that moves across the surface of the disk.

Disk Tools These aren't spanners! Instead, disk tools are a set of software programs that help you monitor the performance of your disk, maintain it, and ensures that it's storing data efficiently and is in tip-top condition. If you look in the Accessories folder of Windows, you'll see the disk tools that are provided: Disk Defragmenter will gather up data that's spread up all over the surface of your disk and stores it neatly; Scan Disk will look at every part of the disk and check it for faults and, if it finds any, will try to fix them. You should run both of these tools around once a month to prevent any problems.

Display Adapter The electronic device that controls what you see on your monitor. The display adapter takes instructions from the PC and converts them into electrical signals that define the color and character shapes you see on your screen. If you have a graphics display adapter – such as an SVGA adapter – fitted in your PC, then this will manage all the high resolution graphics and color and characters that you see on the monitor.

Distance Distance between neurons, calculated from their positions with a distance function.

Distance Function Particular way of calculating distance, such as the Euclidean distance between two vectors.

Distributed Database Defined as consisting of a collection of data with different parts under the control of separate DDBMS running on independent computer systems. All the computers are interconnected and each system has autonomous processing capability, serving local application. Each system participates in the execution of one or more global application. Such applications required data from more than one site.

Dither To smooth out any jagged edges of a curve (for example, in drawing or on a character) by placing shaded pixels between the pixels that make up the curve. Some graphics programs will do this automatically and some high resolution laser printers will do this to improve the quality of the print.

To create a new color by displaying a pattern of colored pixels that appears, to the eye, as a new color. The eye blends the tiny pixels together and is fooled into thinking that this is a new color. For example, a pattern of black and white pixels equally spaced would appear as grey; increase the number of black pixels and the grey darkens.

DOC File name extension for a word processor or information file.

Domain A "logical" region of the Internet. People sometimes refer to them loosely as "sites". Generally, a domain corresponds to an IP address or an area on a host.

Domain Name System (DNS) The naming scheme used in the internet is called the DNS. Each computer name consists of a sequence of alpha-numeric segments separated by periods. For example www.gcwm.in

Domain name	Assigned to
com	Commercial organization
edu	Educational institution
gov	Government organization
mil	Military group
net	Major network support center
org	Organization other than those above
int	International organization
Country codes ex., in for India, us for United States etc.,	A country

DOS This was the standard, most common operating system before Windows arrived. Basically, DOS is just a piece of software that manages how files are stored on the disk. It keeps track of where the files are stored, how big they are, and when they are created. It also provides time and date functions, together with the ability to start other software programs. DOS is controlled through a command line interface, which means that you have to type in words to get it to do something. For example, if you want to see the files stored on a disk, type DIR (short for directory). DOS

is flexible and quick, but is difficult for beginners to use because it's not in the least bit friendly. Windows changes all this by getting rid of the command-line interface and providing a graphical user interface in which you control actions by pointing and clicking with a mouse there's no need to learn or type in command words.

Download To transfer information from an on-line network onto a

user's personal computer. This may be done for conference or e-mail messages which need to be printed, copied to diskette, or simple browed at leisure.

DQDB: Distributed Queue Dual Bus It consists of two unidirectional buses (cables) to which all the computers are connected. Each bus has a head-end, a device that initiates transmission activity. Traffic that is destined for a computer to the right of the sender uses the upper bus. Traffic to the left uses the lower one.

Drag And Drop A feature of graphical operating systems. The system means you can move a highlighted icon or piece of text. For example, if you want to delete a file from the windows desktop, you move the printer to the files icon, click once to highlight the icon, and then press and hold down the left-hand mouse button. You have now picked up the icon and can move it around the desktop. With the mouse button still pressed down, move it on top of the

Recycle Bin icon. The Recycle Bin icon will change color to indicate that it's recognized you want to use it. Now release the mouse button and you've deleted the file using drag and drop.

Driver A special piece of software that sits between windows and a peripheral and translates the instructions from windows into a form that the peripheral can understand. In DOS, before windows arrived, all drivers were loaded when the PC was first switched on from within the CONFIG.SYS file, which is why your screen flashes between text and graphics mode when you first switch on your PC and it loads windows.

Drop-Down Menu A list of options that is displayed beneath a menu bar when you select a particular menu option. For example, if you select the File menu from any windows application, list of further options is displayed beneath the word file. This is a drop-down menu. Used in computerizes to describe information that can be represented by a collection of bits.

Dual–Tone Multi–Frequency (DTMF) The tones produced by pressing keys on a telephone. DTMF, also called Touch–Tone, is often used as a way of sending data to IVRs.

Dynamic Allocation You can define a node's type at compile time, but not actually initialize it (create any variable of that type until run time). We refer to this process as dynamic storage allocation. Dynamic variables can be created or destroyed at time during the execution of the program.

Dynamic Binding Binding means to link the procedure call to the code to be executed in response to the call. Dynamic binding means that the code associated with a given procedure call is not known until the time of the call at runtime.

It is associated with polymorphism and inheritance. A function call associated with a polymorphic reference depends on the dynamic type of that reference.

Dynamic Channel Allocation in LANS and MANS

Station model: consists of N independent stations (computers or terminals), each with a program or user that generates frames for transmission. The probability of a frame being generated in an interval of length Δt is $\lambda\Delta t$, where λ is a constant (the arrival rate of new frames).

Single Channel Assumption: available for all communication. All stations can transmit on it and all can receive from it.

Collision Assumption: if two frames are transmitted simultaneously, they overlap in time and the resulting signal is garbled, called a collision. A collided frame must be transmitted again later. There are no errors other than those granted by collisions.

(a) Continuous Time: Frame transmission can begin at any instant. (b) Slotted Time: Time is divided into discrete intervals (slots). A frame transmission always begins at the start of a slot. A slot may contain 0, 1 or more frames, corresponding to an idle slot a successful transmission or a collision respectively.

(a) Carrier Sense: Stations can tell if the channel is in use before trying to use it. If the channel is sensed as busy, no station will attempt to use it until it goes idle. (b) No Carrier Sense: Stations cannot sense the channel before trying to use it and go ahead and transmit.

Dynamic Hashing Techniques
Dynamic hashing is the solution to the problem that static hash structures have when the number of records to be stored in the file either increases very close to or beyond expectations or perhaps decreases to levels much less than anticipated. With a static structure either insufficient space is available leading to unreasonably high collision rates or too much allocated space is unutilized leading to high overhead in terms of space. With static hashed structures the solution to either of these problems is an incredibly time consuming reorganization of the hashed structure. As the file grows in size the reorganization becomes simply too costly to effect and other solutions must be employed. Thus, we entered the realm of external dynamically hashed structures which can expand and contract as required based upon the access patterns to the hashed structure. So far we have examined only the form of dynamic hashing known as dynamic hashing. In this se of notes we'll continue with a look at two different dynamic hashing techniques called *extendible hashing* and *linear hashing.*

Dynamic Link Library (DLL)
Commonly used file name extension for library files used by a program.

Dynamic Modeling
The dynamic model of a system aims to specify how the state of various objects changes when events occur. An event is something that happens at some time instance.

Dynamic RAM
It tends to lose their charge with time and needs periodic refreshing. Thus, extra control circuitry and interleaving of normal memory access with refreshing operation. Thus, the dynamic RAMs although can be packed more densely yet are more difficult to use than that of static RAMs. In contrast to ferrite

core memory the semiconductor RAMs are volatile in nature.

Dynamic Variable A variable created at run time. The implication of this idea for creating a linked list is obvious. If we can get space for new nodes as we need them, we are no longer required to declare an array large enough to hold the maximum possible number of list elements. The GetNode operation goes out and gets space from the system; the FreeNode operation returns space to the system. We do not need to know in advance how large the list will be. The only limitation is the amount of available memory space.

E

Early Stopping Technique based on dividing the data into three subsets. The first subset is the training set, used for computing the gradient and updating the network weights and biases. The second subset is the validation set. When the validation error increases for a specified number of iterations, the training is stopped, and the weights and biases at the minimum of the validation error are returned. The third subset is the test set. It is used to verify the network design.

EBCDIC (Extended Binary Coded Decimal Interchange Code) A standard code for numeric representation of alphanumeric characters.

E-Cash This method of purchase allows payments for purchase goods by transmitting a number from customer compute to the seller's computer system. These numbers are issued by the bankers which represents the value for the money. These devices are known as digital cash and have monetary value, preservability, interoperability and security.

EDI File Formats EDI creates the following files as a document passes through the system.

Internal Format File (IFF): it contains a single document for a single trading partner. IFF is principally for EDI's own use.

External Format File (EFF): It contains the same data as the IFF translated into the appropriate standard document format.

Transmission File: It contains one or more documents for the same trading partner. Documents of the same type are packaged together in functional group.

The functional group going to one trading partners are packaged into an interchange set. An interchange set contains one or more functional groups of documents with the same sender and receiver.

Educational And Research Network (ERNET) Its foundation was laid in 1987 by the Department of Electronics with the aim to make available an exclusive network for the communication between educational and research institutions of the country. ERNET is a unique and India's first TCP/IP network of its own kind.

Eigen Values It arises in many physical problems. Some of the physical situations where Eigen values are required can be listed: Flexural oscillations of a tapered rod, vibration problems, stability problems, buckling of columns, stability of electrical circuits etc., while trying to analyses the solution to these type of problems, we come across Eigen value problem.

Electronic Data Interchange (EDI) It is the electronic exchange of business documents in a standard, computer process able, universally accepted format between trading partners. EDI is quite different from sending electronic mail, messages or sharing files through a network. In EDI, the computer application of both the sender and the receiver, refer to as Trading Partners (TPs) have to agree upon the format of the business document which is sent as a data file over an electronic messaging services.

Electronic Payment System It is a central part of E-Commerce activities as it deals with the strategies for the payment of goods and services by online customer. Electronic payments also refer to the activity of account settlement where the prompt settlement of payment is crucial. If the debit and credit to the bank account, customer and the company are not settled immediately or suffers due to conventional processing delays, then the entire business chain may be interrupted. Payment and settlement of the business account are the bottleneck in all E-commerce activities. The instruments used to make payments on the Internet are Credit/ Debit cards.

Electronic Purse These devices are like smart card. These wallet size card embedded with micro-programmable microchips which have money value in it. On being purchase a product, its equivalent value is deducted from it.

E-Mail A way of sending and receiving message between users on a network. If you work in an office and all the PCs are

linked in a local area network, you could send messages to each user on the network. If you are connected to the Internet, you can send messages to any other user who is also connected to the Internet. In order to send a message, you'll need special software.

Embed To place an element or object such as text or graphics form one document, file or application into another. Embedding implies the inclusion of all data necessary to maintain or change the format of the element within the new application.

Embedded Commands Computer program instructions the establish and maintain the appearance, position and special characteristics of text or graphics element.

Embedded Object A drawing, chart, spread sheet, sound recording etc. that is imported from another document or file. The embedded object becomes a part of the host file and may be represented graphically, such as for a drawing or spread sheet, or it may be.

Embedded Pointer A link between an embedded object and its source file, such as a link between a chart and the spread sheet form which it was derived.

Emitter Coupled Logic [ECL] ECL is the fastest of all logic families and therefore is used in applications where very high speed is essential because the transistors are used in different amplifier configuration, in which they are never driven into saturation and thereby the storage time is eliminated. Here, rather than switching the transistors from ON to OFF and vice-versa, they are switched between cutoff and active regions.

Emulate To imitate something else. For example, a special piece of software running on an Apple Macintosh can emulate Windows and allow you to run PC programs on a Mac.

Enabled A function or menu item that can be used. If you look at the software you are using, you'll sometimes see some of the options appear in grey rather than black. These are not enabled and you cannot use the option. For example,

if you are using a word processor and have not selected an area of text, the Copy and Cut commands in the Edit menu are shown in grey and cannot be used. If you select an area of text, look at the Edit menu again and you'll see these options now appear in black and have been enabled.

Encapsulation The wrapping up of data and functions (that operate on the data) into a single unit (called class) is known as encapsulation. It is an away to implement data abstraction.

Encoder An **encoder** is a device, circuit, transducer, software program, algorithm or person that converts information from one format or code to another, for the purposes of standardization, speed, secrecy, security or compressions.

E

Encryption	The basis of network security. Encryption encodes network packets to prevent anyone except the intended recipient from accessing the data.
End User	The end user is you! You are the person who will use the program or product that a developer is creating.
Enter	The key on your keyboard. Almost all commands used on a network should be followed by. Also called, or carriage return.
Entity Relationship Diagrams	E-R diagrams basically represent the overall logical structure of a database. The data models of a database represent a collection of conceptual tools for describing data, data relationship, data semantics and consistency constraints. The various data models fall into three important categories: 1. Object-based logical model, 2. Record-based logical model, 3. Physical data model
Environment	The environment is the imaginary space in which you work when you use your PC. When you switch on your PC and it loads DOS or Windows, it creates an environment for you to work in. this can be changed to suit your needs – by defining its characteristics such as color or wallpaper, and by setting up the printer, keyboard and fonts for you to use.
Epoch	Presentation of the set of training (input and/or target) vectors to a network and the calculation of new weights and biases. Note that training vectors can be presented one at a time or all together in a batch.
Ergodic Process	It is a process in which any state can be reached (eventually) from any other state.

Ernet Nodal Centers In order to make the ERNET project successful, government of India set up eight nodal centers in India which are connected to each other through the leased lines. The nodal centers are

Indian Institute of Technology, Mumbai.

Indian Institute of Technology, Kanpur.

Indian Institute of Technology, Kharagpur.

Indian Institute of Technology, Chennai.

Indian Institute of Technology, New Delhi.

Indian Institute of Science, Bangalore.

National Centre for Software Technology, Mumbai

Department of Electronics, New Delhi.

Error The term error is used in two different ways. It refers to the discrepancy between a computed, observed, or measured value and the true, specified, or theoretically correct value. That is, error refers to the difference between the actual output of software and the correct output.

Error Box Or Message A small window that pops up to tell you an error has occurred. For example, if you have tried to do something that the program does not understand, or if an error has occurred in the program.

Error Checking Uploading or downloading transfer check employed to identify errors in data transmission.

Error Guessing The programs often produce incorrect behavior when inputs form some special cases. The reason is that in programs, some combinations of inputs need special treatment, and providing proper handling for these special cases is easily overlooked. For example, in an arithmetic routine, if there is a division and the divisor is zero, some special action has to be taken, which could easily be forgotten by the programmer. These special cases form particularly good test cases, which can reveal errors that will usually not be detected by other test cases.

Error Jumping Special cases will often depend on the data structures and the function of the module. There are no rules to determine special cases, and the tester has to use his intuition and experience to identify such test cases. Consequently, determining special cases is also called error guessing. The tester should play the "devil's advocate" and try to guess the incorrect assumptions the programmer could have made and the situations the programmer could have overlooked or handled incorrectly. Essentially, the tester is trying to identify error-prone situations.

Error Ratio Training parameter used with adaptive learning rate and momentum training of back propagation networks.

Error Tolerance The damage that occurs when the program encounter an error.

Error Vector Difference between networks's output vector in response to an input vector and an associated target output vector.

Esc Key A key on a PC keyboard, in the top left – hand corner that is sometimes used to cancel an action. In Windows pressing the Esc key is the same as selecting the cancel button. If you press Alt – Esc within Windows you will cycle between any program windows that are currently running.

ESP File name extension used for postscript graphics files and that contain vector or bitmapped graphics information.

Ethernet A standard and probably the most popular connection type for Local Area Networks (LANs). It was first developed by Xerox, and later refined by Digital, Intel and Xerox. In an Ethernet configuration, computers are connected by coaxial or twisted – pair cable where they contend for network access using a Carrier Sense Multiple Access with Collision Detection (CSMA/CD) paradigm. Ethernet can transfer information at up to 10 Gigabit-per-second (Gb/s).

Eulerian Paths And Circuits Eulerian path in a graph is defined as a path that traverses each edge in the graph once and only once.

Eulerian circuit is also defined similarly as a circuit that traverses each edge in the graph once and only once.

Evolving Role Of Software The early years – Batch orientation, Limited distribution, and Custom software. Second era – multiuser, Real time, Database, Product software. Third era – Distributed systems, Embedded "intelligence", Low cost hardware, consumer impact. Forth era – powerful desktop systems, object oriented technologies, expert systems, artificial neural networks, parallel computing, network computers.

EXE File The three letter filename extension that indicates that a file is a program and can be run. If you start a DOS window from Windows (or if you are already in DOS) type DIR and you'll see the names of all the files stored in the current directory on your hard disk. To the right of the filename is the 3 letter filename extension that describes the type of file. DOC means document, WAV extension Wave or sound file, EXE means executable-a program file that can be run. To run a file with an EXE extension, just type in its name – you don't need to add the EXE suffix – and press Return.

Execution Efficiency The run – time performance of a program.

Expandability The degree to which architectural, data or procedural design can be extended.

Explorer A program that's supplied with Windows that lets you manage all the files stored on a disk. With Explorer you can copy files, move files from one folder to another, create new folders, and rename or delete files and folders. Explorer can also view folders on other PCs in a network. To start Explorer, click on the Start button, then choose Programs/Explorer.

Export To convert a file its native format to another format so that it can be read by a different program. For example, if you have written a letter in Microsoft Word and want to give it to a friend who uses a Word Perfect for Windows, you need to export the Word document to a Word Perfect format file using the File/Save as option in Word.

Extended ASCII An 8-bit code with 256 combinations. The ASCII code is extended from seven bits to eight bits to include additional graphic symbols.

Extension The three letter code at the end of a file name that Generally indicates the type of format of the file. For Example, a filename in MS-DOS might be Letter 1 with the extension .doc. This is written with a full stop separating the two parts of the name. The three letter extension. doc shows the files is a document. Similarly, .bmp means a bitmap file; .exe means an executable program file and so on.

F

Facilitated Application Specification Techniques (FAST)
The FAST team is comprised of representing from marketing, Software and Hardware Engineering and manufacturing.

Facilitator
A network user who is responsible for a particular conference.

Failure
It is the inability of a system or component to perform a required function according to its specifications. A software failure occurs if the behavior of the software is different from the specified behavior. Failures may be caused by functional or performance factors.

FAT
Stands for File Allocation Table. A special data file that's stored on a disk and contains the name, size, date and location of all the files that are stored on the disk. When you open a document, the word processor asks DOS to open the file. It does this by looking through the file allocation table to find the position on the disk where the file is stored. The FAT is hidden, so you cannot see it. But without it you cannot retrieve any of the information stored on your disk. Sometimes the FAT can get corrupted. To remedy this problem run Scandisk or one of the disk recovery programs such as Norton Disk Doctors.

Fault
It is a condition that causes a system to fail in performing its required function. A fault is the basic reason for software malfunction and is practically synonymous with the commonly used term bug, or the somewhat more general term defect. The term error is also often used to refer to defects.

Fault Tolerance
Fault tolerance requirements can place a major constraint on how the system is

to be designed, as they make the system more complex and expensive. Recovery requirements are often an integral part here, detailing what the system should do if some failure occurs to ensure certain properties.

Fault-Based Testing The object of fault based testing within an object oriented system is to design tests that have a high likelihood of uncovering plausible faults. Because the product or system must conform to customer requirements, the preliminary planning required to perform fault based testing begins with the analysis model. It misses two main types of errors

1. Incorrect Specifications and
2. Interactions among subsystems.

FAX Your PC can send and receive normal faxes, just like an office fax machine. To do this, you'll need a special modem that can handle fax data. If you want to send hand written notes, you will also need a scanner, so letters and graphics created on your PC can be sent directly via the fax modem. If you have a modem that can send and receive faxes, you can control it through Windows or any O.S. if your computer receives a fax, it stored as an image, which you can then view on screen or print out. If you want to send a fax, there are several ways of doing this. The easiest is to install the fax modem as a type of printer. If you want to fax a letter to someone, type the letter in your word processor and select the file/print. You'll see your normal printer listed together with the fax modem. Choose the fax modem and you'll be asked to type in the fax telephone number of the recipient.

Federal Networking Council (FNC) A collection of federal agencies that have heavy interests in federal networks using TCP/IP and the Internet. Representatives from DOD, DOE, DARPA, NSF, and NASA & HHS are the major members of the FNC.

Feed Forward Network Layered network in which each layer only receives inputs from previous layers.

Feedback Network Network with connections from a layer's output to that layer's input. The feedback connection can be direct or pass through several layers.

Fiber Optics In optical technology, to transmit data by pulses of light pulse can be used to signal a 1 bit; the absence of a pulse signals a 0 bit.

Field A heading in record used to identify a piece of data. E.g. the field COUNTRY could identify the piece of data "INDIA".

File A named group of characters or data bits in your computer or on the network. Files in a computer are similar to file folders in a filing cabinet. Such a file is made up of records.

File Format The way the data is stored in a file. For example, every document created in Word for Windows is stored as a Word file with special codes to tell Word how the margins are set up, the fonts that are used, and whether any images are included. Each program stores information in its own format. This means it's difficult to read a file that's been created by a different program from the one you are using. To get around this you can either use the Import function, or one of the standard file formats that let you exchange data between programs.

The type of file, such as picture or text; represented as a suffix at the end of the filename. Examples: text= .txt, Word =.doc,

Excel spreadsheet = .xls, Excel chart = .xlc, Excel workbook = .xlw, Bitmap file =.bmp.

File Manager A program supplied with O.S that lets you manage the files stored on a disk. With File Manager you can copy files, move files from one directory to another, create new directories, and rename or delete files.

File Server A computer designated to store software, courseware, administrative tools and other data on a local or wide area network. It "serves" this information to other computers via the network when users enter their personal access codes.

File Sharing If you have two or more PCs linked together in a network, then you can share files between users. Sometimes only one user will use a file at any particular time, in other cases several users might be looking at a file at the same time. In these cases, the network software needs to be able to allow more than one user to access the same file. To do this there is a special file attribute bit called shareable. When this is set to 1, the file can be shared by more than one user. To set a file attribute bit use the Attrib command from DOS or display the file's Properties Window. If you are not connected to a network, you don't need to worry about file sharing.

File Transfer Protocol (FTP) The most widely used way of downloading and uploading (getting and putting) files across an Internet connection. The FTP is a standardized way to connect computers so that files can share between them easily. There is a set of commands in FTP for making and changing directories, transferring, copying, moving, and deleting files. Formerly, all FTP connections were text based, but graphical applications are now available that make FTP commands as easy as dragging and dropping. Numerous FTP clients exist for a number of platforms.

Fillmore's Case Grammar Fillmore's is the notation of using case to extract the meaning of sentence. He extended the trans formal grammar of Chomskey focusing more on semantic sentence. It is using the case grammar Fillmore suggested case grammar. It is refined form of case grammar.

Find Useful features of Windows that will search any disk drive-on your PC or of you are on a network, on any other PC on that network for a particular file.

Finger A UNIX command that shows information about a user or group of users on the Internet. When executed, the Finger command usually returns the user's real name, whether or not they have unread mail, and the time and date of their last login. Finger also displays two files (if they exist) located in the home directory of the user you fingered. These two files (the .PLAN and the .PROJECT files) are simply ASCII text files that can be entered by the user to display any information upon being fingered.

Firmware The firmware is a midway between hardware and software. Firmware, in comparison to hardware is easier to design, whereas in to comparison to software, is difficult to write.

First Normalization Form (1-NF) A relation scheme is said to be 1NF is the values on the domain of each attributes of the relation are atomic.

FIRST-COME-FIRST SERVED SCHEDULING Scheduling Algorithm, but it can cause short jobs to wait for very long jobs

F

Flame A negative response to an email message or news group posting. If you post an article or send an email to an audience that deems your message inappropriate, expect to get flamed. The most common recipients of flames are users who post commercial messages in public forums, those who post adult material in non-adult areas of the Internet, and users who post or send make racial or gender-biased comments. The worst sort of flame is known as a mail-bomb, which occurs when the user being flamed open his or her email and receives a flood of letters with unusually long file attachments' that make his or her computer crash.

Flash Memory The major difference between the flash memory and EE-PROM is in the erasure procedure: the EE-PROM can be erased at a register level, but the flash memory must be erased either in its entirety or at the sector (block) level. These memory chips can be erased and programmed at least a million times.

Flat Screen Older monitors had a curved front to the display which meant that the image could appear distorted at the edges especially if you were trying to display lines or drawings. To provide a clearer, sharper image that is not distorted, monitors are now made with a flatter front. This is not quite as easy as it might sound, and requires complex glass blowing equipment and electronics. If you want to view graphics or drawings as accurately as possible, try to choose a monitor with the flattest screen.

Flatbed Scanner A type of scanner that looks like a small photocopier, you open the lid and place the image face down on a sheet of glass. Close the lid and the scan-head is moved across the entire sheet by accurate motors, converting the image into a graphics file that you can view on your PC. Flatbed scanners are more accurate than hand-held scanners and are normally more expensive.

Fletcher-Reeves Update Method for computing a set of conjugate directions. These directions are used as search directions as part of a conjugate gradient optimization procedure.

Flip Flops A flip flop is a binary cell which can store a bit of information. It is a simplest form of sequential circuit.

Flip-Flops A flip-flop is a memory element that stores binary digit as a low or high voltage. Flip flops are classified as 1. T Flip-Flop, 2. R-S Flip-Flop, 3. Clocked S and R Flip-Flop, 4. J-K Flip-Flop.

Floppy Disk A portable storage device that stores information on a thin, flexible disk. The disk is coated with a magnetic material. The information is stored on the disk as a series of magnetic signals using a disk drive. The flexible disk is protected from grubby fingers in a rigid plastic case with a sliding window on one side to allow the disk drive access to the surface of the disk.

Font A set of characters in the same typeface. For example, labels in Windows are normally displayed in a font called Helvetica or Arial. The characters do not have serifs (the pointy bits on the edges of letters). Windows has True Type fonts that can be printed and displayed in almost any size, and printer fonts that can be printed in predefined sizes.

Foreign Key A non-key attribute, whose values are derived from the primary key of some other table, is known as foreign key in its current table.

Formants To identify these formants here a brief discussion to the speech production in the human body is given: The three main cavities of the speech production system are nasal, oral, and pharyngeal forming the main acoustic filter, The form and shape of the vocal and nasal tracts change continuously with time, creating an acoustic filter with time-varying frequency response. As air from the lungs travels through the tracts, the frequency spectrum is shaped by the frequency selectivity of these tracts. The resonance frequencies of the vocal tract tube are called formant frequencies or simply formants. Which depend on the shape and dimensions of the vocal tract? The speed by which the cords open and close is unique for each individual and define the feature and personality of the particular voice

Format To arrange text, define margins and columns, and include special fonts in a word processor or DTP program.

Format A Disk To prepare a new disk so files can be stored on it. You need to format any disk before you use it: use Format from File Manager or Explorer.

Fourth Normal Form It deals with the situation that arises in case of dependencies of set of entities.

Fragmentation Sec in memory fragmentation

Free Net A network system made up of community based bulletin board systems with email, information services, interactive communications, and conferencing. They are usually funded and operated by individuals or organizations much like public television.

Free net providers are part of the National Public Telecommuting Network (NPTN), a Cleveland-based organization that works to make computer networking services as freely available as public libraries.

Freeware Software that is distributed for free, with no license fee.

Frequency Division Multiplexing (Fdm) FDM involves translation of the speech signal from the frequency band 300-3400 Hz to a higher frequency band. Each channel is translated to a different band and then all the channels are combined to form a frequency division multiplexed signal. In FDM, the speech channels are stacked at intervals of 4 KHz to provide a guard band between adjacent channels.

Front End The part of a software program that a user sees and interacts with. The front end has to be carefully designed to be clear and straightforward to use.

Full Duplex Communication providing simultaneous sending and receiving.

Full Text Search To carry out a search for a word or item through the entire text of a database or a multimedia application rather than limit the search to a particular chapter or field.

Function Approximation Task performed by a network trained to respond to inputs with an approximation of a desired function.

Function Key PCs all have at least 12 function keys that run along the top of the keyboard. These have different uses according to different applications. However most use the F1 key to display on-screen help.

Function of O.S Job management, Batch processing, on-line processing, Data management, virtual storage, I/P-O/P management.

FURPS Functionality, Usability, Reliability, Performance and Supportability.

G

Garbage Collection In computer science, **garbage collection (GC)** is a form of automatic memory management. The *garbage collector*, or just *collector*, attempts to reclaim garbage, or memory occupied by objects that are no longer in use by the program. Garbage collection was invented by John McCarthy around 1959 to solve problems in Lisp. Garbage collection is often portrayed as the opposite of manual memory management, which requires the programmer to specify which objects to deallocate and return to the memory system. However, many systems use a combination of approaches, including other techniques such as stack allocation and region inference.

Gateway A kind of "go-between", device or program that passes information between networks that normally couldn't communicate. What used to be called a gateway is now called a router. Not to be confused with a protocol converter.

Gateway It is generally software installed within a router. It operates in all seven layers of the OSI model. It must adjust the data rate, size and format as well. Gateway is used for connecting two dissimilar network means a gateway can accepts and transfer data packet between different networks, it is protocol converter.

Generality The breadth of potential application of program components.

Generalization Attribute of a network whose output for a new input vector tends to be close to outputs for similar input vectors in its training set.

Generalization It is an abstraction for sharing similarities among classes while preserving their differences.

It is the relationship between a class and one or more refined versions of it. The class being refined is called the super class and each refined version is called a subclass.

Generalized Regression Network Approximates a continuous function to an arbitrary accuracy, given a sufficient number of hidden neurons.

Generic Something that is compatible with a whole family of hardware or software products from one manufacturer.

GIF File Stands for Graphics Interface Format. A commonly used format for storing images and bitmapped color graphics. Originally developed for the CompuServe online system, but now one of the most popular formats for images stored on the Internet. Most paint program can read and write to the .gif file format.

Gigabyte (Gb) 1000 Megabytes.

Gini Coefficient Measures The Gini coefficient measures the inequality among values of a frequency distribution (for example levels of income). A Gini coefficient of zero expresses perfect equality where all values are the same (for example, where everyone has an exactly equal income). A Gini coefficient of one (100 on the percentile scale) expresses maximal inequality among values (for example where only one person has all the income)

Gini Index A measurement of the income distribution of a country's residents. This number, which ranges between 0 and 1 and is based on residents' net income, helps define the gap between the rich and the poor, with 0 representing perfect equality and 1 representing perfect inequality.

G

GIS (Geographical Information System)

Main concepts of GIS is

It is a data visualization technology that captures, stores, checks and integrates, manipulates, displays data using digitized maps.

In GIS, every record or digital object has an identified geographic location. By integrating maps with geographic locations and other databases, users can generate information for planning, problem solving and decision making.

GIS helps organizations to increase productivity and quality of its decisions. Data like, location of branch offices, can be superimposed on a map using bullets and colors.

GIS is a more sophisticated way for organizations to gather wide range of information and display it on computer generated maps.

GIS generally used for geographical surveys, can be applied to business and corporate world and almost all functional areas of business.

It is a very important tool used for information sharing between various departments on basis of raw material, production etc.

GKS : Graphical Kernel System

Grammar- A grammar G is defined as a quadruple G= (V, T, S, P) where 'v' is a finite set of objects called variables, 'T' is a finite set of objects called terminal symbols. 'S' belongs to 'V' is a special symbol called the start variable, 'p' is a finite set of productions.

Glass Box Testing

See White Box Testing.

Global Minimum Lowest value of a function over the entire range of its input parameters. Gradient descent methods adjust weights and biases in order to find the global minimum of error for a network.

Golden Section Search Linear search that does not require the calculation of the slope. The interval containing the minimum of the performance is subdivided at each iteration of the search, and one subdivision is eliminated at each iteration.

Gopher An information search and retrieval tool used widely for research. Gopher information is stored hierarchically on computers across the Internet. It uses a simple protocol that allows a client to access information from a multitude of numerous Gopher servers at one time, creating what's known as gopher space. The most common search tools in gopher are Veronica and Jug head. A gopher client exits for most platforms.

Gopher The Gopher technology was invented at the University of Minnesota, whose mascot is, not surprisingly, the Golden Gopher. The gopher system allows people to search for and retrieve information using a text interface. The technology is based on a client-server structure, where a gopher client program is used to search gopher servers. These servers can store documents, articles, programs, and other information. Instead of hyperlinks, the gopher interface uses menus of links to other documents and programs.

The University of Minnesota began a licensing program for the gopher technology in 1993 as the use of gopher was spreading rapidly over the Internet. However, this was around the same time that the World Wide Web was introduced. Because the Web used hypertext and images, it soon became the preferred way to search and browse for information. While there are still servers and client programs that use gopher technology, their use is not nearly as widespread as the Web.

Gopher Space Where you are when you're using a Gopher program.

Gradient Descent Process of making changes to weights and biases, where the changes are proportional to the derivatives of network error with respect to those weights and biases. This is done to minimize network error.

Grammar A file that contains a list of words and phrases to be recognized by a speech application. Grammars may also contain bits of programming logic to aid the application. All of the active grammar words make up the vocabulary.

Graph Matrices It is a square matrix whose size (i.e., number of rows and columns) is equal to the number of nodes on the flow graph. To develop a software tool that assists in basis path testing, a data structure, called a graph matrix, can be quite useful.

Graphical User Interface (GUI) The official definition is rather dry: the interface between an operating system or a program and the person using it. This actually means a way of representing files, functions and folders with little images called icons. Windows is a GUI that makes it easier to operate a PC.

Graphics Computer generated art and illustrations.

Graphics Accelerator A special card that fits inside your computer and uses a dedicated processor chip to speed up the action of drawing lines and images on the screen. In normal PC, the main processor chip has to carry out all the calculations to display a line on screen, all at the same time looking after the keyboard, mouse, disk drive and memory. By adding a graphics accelerator card you can speed up the reaction time of graphics software such as Windows, CAD or Paint programs, as the dedicated processor takes over the job of handling the graphics.

Greeked Text Characters that are displayed as a line rather than individual characters. This is often used by DTP programs when displaying text in a very small type size. Greeked text is only meant to give an impression of the characters rather than a readable display, when you just want to preview an entire page to get an idea of what it looks like.

Greibach Normal Form Here we put restrictions not on the length of the right sides of production, but on the positions in which terminals and variables can appear. Arguments justifying Greibach Normal Form are a little complicated and not very transparent. A Context-Free Grammar is said to be Greibach Normal Form if all productions have the form $A \rightarrow ax$, where $a \rightarrow T$ and $x \rightarrow v^*$

Grid Matrixes of evenly spaced horizontal and vertical lines that help you align and measure drawings. The grid lines are not printed and serve only as a guide for drawing.

Grid Snap A feature of drawing and DTP applications that you will, when you are drawing a line or image, automatically limit the position of the cursor to a point on the grid, making it easier to align drawings and lines.

G

grXML A way of writing SRGS grammars in XML. It is a standard format that is less readable by humans than ABNF grammars, but is used widely by grammar editing tools.

Gutter The blank space between two adjacent columns of text.

Blank space or margin between two facing pages.

H

Hacker Originally someone who was fascinated by computers and tried to program them as efficiently as possible or explore how they worked. Now normally used to refer to someone who is trying to break into a secure computer system for criminal purposes, such as someone trying to discover a way into a bank.

Half Duplex Communication that alternates between sending and receiving.

Halstead's Measure Halstead's complexity measure focused on the internal complexity of a module, as does McCabe's complexity measure. In Halstead's Measure, a module's connection with its environment is reflected in terms of operands and operators. A call to another module is considered an operator, and all the parameters are considered operands of this operator.

Hamiltonian Paths It is defined to be a path that passes through each of the vertices in a graph exactly once.

Hand Held Scanner A small device that plugs into controller card in your PC. The scanner contains a row of light sensitive cells along its bottom surface. When you drag the scanner over an image, it reads the amount of light reflected from the image or photograph and converts this into a form, which can be displayed on your PC. When you buy a hand held scanner it normally comes with the special controller card that plugs inside your PC.

Handle In a graphics or DTP program, a small square that's displayed on the edge of the frame, object or image. If you move the mouse pointer over the handle and click and drag with the mouse, you will resize or move it.

H

Handshaking A procedure performed by modems, terminals, and computers to verify that communication has been correctly established.

Hang A slang term that means your computer has stopped responding because of a temporary fault. Some programs which are not tested thoroughly are liable to stop at unpredictable times and hang the computer. This means that you cannot do anything else except switch off your PC and start again.

Hard-Limit Transfer Function Transfer function that maps inputs greater than or equal to 0 to 1, and all other values to 0.

Hash Addressing Or Scatter Storage Principle: Given that we may access the data through a number of keys Ki, then the address of the data in store is located through a key transformation function f which when applied to Ki evaluates to give the address of the associated data. We are assuming here that with each key is associated only one data item. Also for convenience we will assume that each record (data and key) fits into one location, whose address is in the image space of f. The addresses given by the application of f to the keys Ki are called the hash addresses and f is called a hashing function. Ideally f should be such that it spreads the hash addresses uniformly over the available storage. Of course this would be achieved if the function were one-to-one. Unfortunately this cannot be so because the range of possible key values is usually considerably larger than the range of the available storage addresses. Therefore, given any hashing function we have to contend with the fact that two distinct keys Ki and Kj are likely to map to the same address $f(K_i)$ $(=f(K_j))$.

Hashing File Organization In this organization, a hash function is computed on some attribute of each record. The result of the hash function specifies in which block of the record should be placed.

HEAP File Organization In this organization, any record can be placed anywhere in the file where there is space for the record. There is no ordering of records. Typically, there is a single file for each relation.

Hebb Learning Rule Historically the first proposed learning rule for neurons. Weights are adjusted proportional to the product of the outputs of pre- and post-weight neurons.

Hidden Layer Layer of a network that is not connected to the network output (for instance, the first layer of a two-layer feed-forward network).

Hierarchical Data Model In a hierarchical data model and relationship among data are represented by records and links in a tree structure rather than arbitrary graphs.

Home Neuron Neuron at the center of a neighborhood.

Host Name The name given a host computer connected to the internet.

Host Address The address of a host computer on the internet.

Hot Key a way of selecting a menu option or command by pressing two or more keys at the same time. for example , instead of selecting the File/Save menu option , mist Windows programs use a hot key shortcut of ALT-S(the Alt key and the S key pressed at the same time) to do the same thing . Another useful hot key shortcut is Alt-F4, which will quit any Windows program.

Hotspot In a multimedia title, an area of an image that does something if you move the mouse pointer on to it and click on the mouse button. Normally, you can tell that there is a hotspot in an image because the mouse pointer changes shape from an arrow to a hand. For example, if the multimedia title displayed a picture of a guitar, there could be a hotspot over each string, which would play the sound of the string being plucked.

Hsv Color Model Uses color descriptions that have a more intuitive appeal to a user to give a color specification, a user selects a spectral color and the amounts of white and black that is to be added to obtain different shades, tints and tones. Color parameters in this model are Here (H), Saturation (S) and Value (V).

HTML Stands for Hyper Text Markup Language. A series of special codes that defines the typeface and style that should be used when displaying the text and also allow hypertext links to other parts of the documents or to other documents. HTML is used to create documents for the graphical part of the internet, the World Wide Web. A document coded in HTML can be displayed on any viewer software that understands HTML, such as Mosaic or Netscape Navigator.

Hub Hub is a central controller that controls the traffic on the network. Basically its 2 types

Active Hub: an active hub works as a repeater which is a hardware device that regenerates the received bit pattern before sending them out.

Passive Hub: A passive hub is a simple hardware device which provides a simple physical connection between the attached devices.

Hybrid Bisection Cubic Search Line search that combines bisection and cubic interpolation.

Hyperlinks A hyperlinks is a string that appears in a different color from the rest of the text. When the mouse pointer is over a hyperlink. The pointer turns into a finger or other pointer. When you click the mouse button over a hyperlink, the browser requests and display another document.

Hypermedia The combination of hypertext and multimedia in an online document.

Hyperterminal Communication program that are included with Windows and allows you call a remote computer via a modem and transfer files. It's not meant to be used to access the internet. It's more useful when used to access bulletin boards or other online services.

Hypertext A type of text that allows embedded links to other documents. Clicking on or selecting a hypertext link displays another document or selection of a document. Most World Wide Web documents contain hypertext.

Hytime The Hypermedia / Time-based structure language is an ISO standard for the representation of open hypermedia document and is an application of SGML. Like SGML it does not specify the document content, but provides a standard way in which different types of information can be combined. It is not a DTD, but provides guidelines for DTDs. For ex., the Standard Music Description Language (SMDL) is an application of HyTime.

I

IANA(Internet Assigned Numbers Authority) The central registry for various Internet protocol parameters, such as port, protocol and enterprise, and options, codes and types. The currently assigned values are listed in the Assigned Numbers documents.

I-Beam Cursor A flashing cursor shaped like a capital I used to indicate that you can edit text on screen. If you use a Windows word processor, the mouse pointer turns into an I-beam cursor when you move it over the main page and returns to an arrow shape when you move it over the menu bar or other controls.

IBM Compatible Computers Computers that use the same software as the computers introduced by the IBM Corporation in the early 80's. These computers are manufactured by many companies and are sometimes referred to as "clones".

ICI Interface control information

Icon A small picture displayed on screen to identify a command or file. Many word processors use an icon of a magnifying glass on a button to indicate that it will start a search function. In Windows, each application you install has its own icon and its data files often use the same icon.

IDU : Interface Data Unit In order for two layers to exchange information, there has to be an agreed upon set of rules about the interface.

IEEE Institute of Electrical and Electronics Engineers

Image Editor Software that lets you edit, change or paint new parts of an image. Professional designers might use an image editor to remove any blemishes from a photograph. Windows has its own basic image editor called Paint, stored in the Accessories folder.

Image Processing It is techniques used to modify or interpret existing pictures, such as photographs and TV screen. Two principal applications of the image process are (1) improving picture quality and (2) Machine perception of visual information as used in robotics.

Image Scanners Drawing, graphs, color and black and white photos, or text can be stored for computer processing with an image scanner by passing an optical scanning mechanics, over the information to be stored. The gradations of grass scale or color are then recorded and stored in an array

Import The function in an application that allows you to use a data file produced by another program and stored in another format. For example, if you use Microsoft World and want to read a document written with WordPerfect, you will need to choose the import menu option in Word and tell Word that it should convert the WordPerfect codes to native Word codes and formats. The opposite is called Export.

Index An "index" is a list of the messages contained in a conference or a mail folder. Indexes generally show the date of the message, its title (or subject), the name of the user who wrote it, and an indication (with a "*" marker) of whether you have read that message.

Indexing In order to allow fast random access to records and a file, in index structure is used. Each index structure is associated with a particular search key. If the file is sequentially ordered and if we choose to include several indices on different search keys, the index search key specifies the sequential order of the file is the primary index. The search key of a primary index is usually the primary key. There are two types of indices

1. Sparse Index
2. Dense Index.

Index-Sequential Files

An index-sequential file is an inverted file in which for every keyword K_i, we have $n_i = h_i = 1$ and $a_{11} < a_{21} \ldots < a_{m1}$. This situation can only arise if each record has just one unique keyword, or one unique attribute-value. In practice therefore, this set of records may be order sequentially by a key. Each key value appears in the directory with the associated address of its record. An obvious interpretation of a key of this kind would be the record number.

Inference Process

The inference engine accepts user input queries and responses to questions through the I/O interface and uses this dynamic information together with the static knowledge (the rules and facts) stored in the knowledge base. The knowledge in knowledge base is used to derive conclusions about the current case or situation as presented by the user's input.

The inferring process is carried out recursively in three stages: match, select and execute.

Inherently Ambiguous

If 'L' is a context free language for which there exists an unambiguous grammar, then L is said to be unambiguous, if every grammar that generates L is ambiguous, then the language is called inherently ambiguous.

Inheritance

It is the process by which objects of one class acquire properties of objects of another class. In other words. A class is derived from the base class is called derived class and this concept is called inheritance. A class which derive from the another class is called derived class. A class which derived another class is called base class.

Initialization Process of setting the network weights and biases to their original values.

Input To transfer information into a computer. If you type text on your keyboard you are inputting data into the computer. Other examples are using a scanner or using a mouse to draw on screen.

Input / Output Register This register is used to communicate with the input / output devices. All input information such as instructions and data is transferred to this register by an input device. Similarly, all output information to be transferred to an output device is found in this register.

Input Devices Mouse, trackball, space ball, joystick, digitizer, dials and button boxes, data gloves, touch panels, image scanners OCR, MICR, OMR, Bar Code Reader, voice systems and so on.

Input Layer Layer of neurons receiving inputs directly from outside the network.

Input Space Range of all possible input vectors.

Input Vector Vector presented to the network.

Input Weight Vector Row vector of weights going to a neuron.

Input Weights Weights connecting network inputs to layers.

INS Key A special key on a PC that switches the typing mode between insert and overwrite. If you are in over-write mode, any existing characters will be overwritten with the new text you type in. If you are in insert mode, any existing characters are moved along automatically to make space for the new characters. Most word processors tell you which mode you are in by displaying OVR for overwrite and INS for insert in the status bar at the bottom of the screen.

I

Insertion Sort It is a simple sorting algorithm that builds the final sorted array (or list) one item at a time. It is much less efficient on large lists than more advanced algorithms such as quicksort, heap sort, or merge sort. However, insertion sort provides several advantages:

Simple implementation

Efficient for (quite) small data sets

Adaptive (i.e., efficient) for data sets that are already substantially sorted: the time complexity is $O(n + d)$, where d is the number of inversions

More efficient in practice than most other simple quadratic (i.e., $O(n^2)$) algorithms such as selection sort or bubble sort; the best case (nearly sorted input) is $O(n)$

Stable; i.e., does not change the relative order of elements with equal keys

In-place; i.e., only requires a constant amount O(1) of additional memory space

Online; i.e., can sort a list as it receives it

Insertion Time The time it takes to insert a new data item. This includes the time it takes to find the correct place to insert the new data item as well as the time it takes to update the index structure.

Install The steps involved in copying and setting up an application program on your hard disk. The steps include copying the files from the floppy disks or CD-ROM (on which the application is sold) on to your hard disk, then configuring the options for your requirements.

Instruction Decoder In CPU design, the instruction decoder is the part of the CPU that converts the bits stored in the instruction register – or, in CPUs that have microcode, the microinstruction – into the control signals that control the other parts of the CPU.

A simple CPU with 8 registers may use 3-to-8 logic decoders inside the instruction decoder to select two source registers of the register file to feed into the ALU as well as the destination register to accept the output of the ALU. A typical CPU instruction decoder also includes several other things.

Instructions Register It holds the current instruction that is being executed. As soon as the instructions are stored in this register, the operation part and the address part of the instructions are separated. The address part of the instruction is sent to the MAR while its operation part is sent to the control section where it is decoded and interpreted and ultimately command signals are generated to carry out the task specified by the instruction.

Instrumentation The degree to which the program monitors its own operation and identifies errors that do occur.

Integration Testing It is a systematic technique for constructing the program structure while conducting tests to uncover errors associated with interfacing. The objective is to take unit tested modules and build a program structure that has conforms to the design.

Integrity Mechanisms (Secret Key0 The following techniques are used to ensure the integrity of data against accidental damage. Parity bits, Checksums and Cyclic Redundancy Checks (CRCs). To use such techniques, sender computers, a small integer value as a function of the data in a packet. The receiver recomputed the function from the data that arrives and compares the result to the value that the sender computed.

A checksum or CRC cannot absolutely guarantee data integrity for two reasons:

If malfunctioning hardware changes the value of a checksum as well as the value of the data, it is possible for the altered checksum to be valid for the altered data.

If data changes result from a planned attack, the attacker can create a valid checksum for the altered data.

Interactive A multimedia title that allows the user to control progress through the book. Instead of the software showing page one, then two and so on, the user can move around and click on hypertext links and hotspot that move him around the book in a random order.

Interactive Processing Computer processing that requires input from the user at certain points in the procedure.

Interactive Program An application that responds to each user command as it is entered, and then waits for next command.

Interactive System A computer system that provides a means of communication between the operating system and the user or peripherals.

Interactive Voice Response (IVR) An automated system that allows callers to interact with a computer, using a telephone (or VOIP). An IVR may use speech recognition, DTMF, or a combination of the two.

Interface (See GUI)

Internal Processor Memories These consist of the small set of high speed registers which are internal to a processor and are used as temporary locations where actual processing is done.

Internet An international network that links thousands of computers using telephone and cable links. Users connect to server computers, which are rather like a local phone exchange: you use a modem to connect to the server from home and so access the entire network. You can send email over the Internet and transfer files and text from a PC in London to another in New York, all for the price of a local phone call. To get on to the Internet, you'll need a modem and an account with a server, normally called a service provider.

Internet Protocol(IP) An industry standard, connectionless, best-effort packet switching protocol used as the network layer in the TCP/IP Protocol Suite.

Internet Society (ISOC) A non-profit, professional organization that supports the technical evolution of the internet and stimulates the interest of members of the scientific and academic communities, industry, and the public regarding technology and the applications of the internet. The ISOC also promotes the development of new applications for the internet by publishing a quarterly newsletter, the Internet Society News, and holding an annual conference, called INET.

InterNIC Meaning internet information center, InterNIC is the combined name for the providers of registration, information, and database services to the internet. InterNIC is who you contact if you want to register a domain name on the internet.

Interrupts Interrupts is defined loosely to any exceptional event that causes CPU to temporarily transfer its control from currently executing program to a different program which provide service to the exceptional event. An interrupt may be generated by a number of sources which may be either internal or external to the CPU.

I

Interviewing

The primary purpose of interviewing is to obtain both quantitative and qualitative data regarding user requirements, policies, procedures and practices. The key to a successful interview is to observe good manners, have an open mind, and encourage the person being interviewed to reveal all important details.

Inverted File Structure

An inverted file is a file structure in which every list contains only one record. Remember that a list is defined with respect to a keyword K, so every K-list contains only one record. This implies that the directory will be such that $n_i = h_i$ for all i, that is, the number of records containing K_i will equal the number of K_i -lists. So the directory will have an address for each record containing K_i. For document retrieval this means that given a keyword we can immediately locate the addresses of all the documents containing that keyword. The definition of inverted files does not require that the addresses in the directory are in any order. However, to facilitate operations such as conjunction ('and') and disjunction ('or') on any two inverted lists, the addresses are normally kept in record number order. This means that 'and' and 'or' operations can be performed with one pass through both lists. The penalty we pay is of course that the inverted file becomes slower to update.

IP Address (Internet Protocol Address)

The 32-bit address defined by the Internet Protocol. Every resource on the Internet has a unique numerical IP address, represented in dotted decimal notation. IP address is the closest thing the Internet has to phone numbers. When you "call" that number (using any number of connection methods such as FTP, HTTP, Gopher, etc.) you get connected to the computer to which that IP address is assigned.

IRC The worldwide party line of the '90s. IRC allows multiple users to converse in real time on different channels. Channels (which have a # sign preceding their name) vary in traffic and connect. Channel operators (or ops) moderate the conversation, and have the ability to "kick" people from channels, or even ban them actions warrant it. IRC clients are available for nearly all platforms.

ISDN (Integrated Services Digital Network) A relatively new technology, which combines voice and digital network services in a single medium. ISDN makes it possible for communications carries to offer their customer's digital data services as well as voice connections through a single line. CCITT defines the standards relating to ISDN.

ISO 9000 Quality Standards A quality assurance system may be defined as the organizational structure, responsibilities, procedures, processer and resources for implementing quality management. ISO 9000 describes quality assurance elements in generic terms that can be applied to any business regardless of the products or services offered.

Iso 9001 Standard It is the quality assurance standard that applies to software engineering. The standard contains 20 requirements that must be present for an effective quality assurance system.

1.management responsibility

2.quality system

3.control review

4.design control

5.document and data control

6.purchasing

7.control of customer supplied product
8.product identification and traceability
9.process control
10.inspection and testing
11.control of inspection, measuring and test equipment 12.inspection and test status
13.control of non-conforming product
14.corrective and preventive action
15.handling, storage, packaging, preservation and delivery
16. control of quality records
17. Internal quality audits
18.training
19.servicing
20.statistical techniques

Isolated-Word System An isolated-word system operates on single words at a time - requiring a pause between saying each word. This is the simplest form of recognition to perform because the end points are easier to find and the pronunciation of a word tends not affect others. Thus, because the occurrences of words are more consistent they are easier to recognize.

ISP Information strategy planning. Objectives of ISP are 1.to define strategic business objectives and goals 2.to isolate the critical success factors that will enable the business to achieve these goals and objectives 3.to analyze the impact of technology and automation on the goals and objectives 4.to analyze existing information to determine its role in achieving goals and objectives.

ISP (Internet Service Provider) An ISP is a company that maintains a network that is linked to the internet via a dedicated communication line, usually a high-speed link known as a T1. An ISP offers use of its dedicated communication lines to companies or individuals (like me) who can't afford $1,300 a month for direct connection. Using a modem, you can dial up to a service provider whose computers will connect you to the Internet, typically for a fee.

Iterative Enhancement Model In this model, it has been proposed that the changes in the software system throughout its lifetime are an iterative process. Originally proposed as a development model but well suited to maintenance, the motivation for this was the environment where requirements were not fully understood and a full system could not be built.

IXC Interexchange Carrier

J

Jacobian Matrix Contains the first derivatives of the network errors with respect to the weights and biases.

Jacobson Method Also called OOSE. It process

1. Identify the users of the system and their overall responsibilities
2. Build a requirements model.
3. Build analysis model.

Jaggies Slang term for the jagged edges that you'll see along the sides of curves, graphics or round characters. Jaggies occur because the printer can only print individual dots rather than smooth lines.

Java Applets JAVA programs that work on web pages are called Applets. They are embedded in HTML files. To use an applet, one needs to have a JAVA enable web browser, which interprets the byte code. Applets can also be used to add buttons and input fields to web pages.

Jitter A fault on a monitor that causes annoying, tiny movements of characters.

Joystick It a pointing device and is used for the same purpose as a mouse. In joystick, a stick can be moved right, left, forward or backward. The electronics in the joystick measures the movement of the stick from its central position and sends the information for processing. Joystick is used for games programs.

JPEG (Joint Photographic Experts Group) A standard you come across if you use graphic images. JPEG is a complex way of joining images in a compressed format so they take up a much less disk space.

Jukebox

A jukebox is a sophisticated CD-ROM drive that can hold several CD-ROM discs and select the correct disc when required.

Jukeboxes are not meant for just one user; they connect to a network and can contain hundreds of standard CD-ROM discs that many users need to an access.

K

K – Means The K-means algorithm partitions the T feature vectors into M centroids. The algorithm first randomly chooses M cluster-centroids among the T feature vectors. Then each feature vector is assigned to the nearest centroid, and the new centroids are calculated for the new clusters. This procedure is continued until a stopping criterion is met, that is the mean square error between the feature vectors and the cluster-centroids is below a certain threshold or there is no more change in the cluster-center assignment

Karnaugh Maps It is a simple direct approach of simplification of logic expressions. It is a convenient way of representing and simplifying Boolean function of 4 to 6 variables.

Kermit A communication protocol that allows you to transfer files between your computer and on-line network systems. Kermit has built-in error correction and can handle binary (non-text).

Key (Primary, Candidate, Super) Is a property of the entity set, rather than of the individual entities? Any two individual entities in the set are prohibited from having the same value on the key attributes at the same time. The designation of a key represents a constraint in the real-world enterprise being modeled.

Key Combination A combination of two or more keys that carry out a function when pressed together. For example, the key combination Alt-S normally saves the file you are working on in any Windows program, and Alt-F4 will exit the program you are using.

Keyboard

On the keyboard each key is attached to a spring and a tiny electrical switch. When you press a key, the switch closes and sends a signal to the PC. In addition to the main characters, there is a row of 12 function keys along the top of the keyboard. These do different things according to the program you are using. The only standard is thatF1 will normally display Help. If you hold down a key, the character appears once then, after a short delay, the character is repeated until you lift off the key.

KHZ

1) A measure of the frequency of a sound. Once KHz (or kilohertz) is equal to 1,000 cycles per second. The higher the number, the higher pitched the sound. Normal speech has a very limited frequency range-mostly between 300Hz and 2.4 KHz. Music and other sounds can be heard at far higher lower frequencies. 2) You will also see KHz mentioned in the specification of a soundcard. This can define two separate functions. The first is the range of the frequencies the soundcard can output. The second is the frequency at which the soundcard takes samples of a sound when recording it on to your disk. A soundcard looks at the level of sound thousands of times each second and so builds up a picture of it. The more times it takes a sample, the more accurate the recording. The number of times the soundcard takes a sample per second is described in KHz. A good soundcard should cope with 22 KHz or 44 KHz samples.

K

Kilobyte (Kb)	A measure of the capacity of a storage device that is usually written as Kb. A Kb is equal to 1,024 bytes. If you want to check the size of a file, highlight the file name in program manager in Windows. The size of a file is displayed after the file name. Although 1Kb is actually equal to 1,024 bytes, many people use to mean 1,000 bytes. The reason that 1Kb has 1,024 bytes is that it is equal to two to the power of 10-remender that PCs work in a binary, base 2.
Knot Count	A method for quantifying complexity based on the locations of the control transfers of the program has been proposed in 1985. It was designed largely for FORTRAN programs, where explicit transfer of control is shown by the use of goto statements. A programmer, to understand a given program, typically draws arrows from the point of control transfer to its destination, helping to create a mental picture of the program and the control transfers in it. According to this metric, the more intertwined these arrows become, the more complex the program. This notion is captured in the concept of a "kont".
Kohonen Learning Rule	Learning rule that trains a selected neuron's weight vectors to take on the values of the current input vector.

L

Label There are two ways of labeling a floppy disk. The first is to stick a paper label on it. The second is to give the disk an electronic label. This is called the volume name. If you want to give a short description to a floppy disk (which will appear in My computer window) highlight the floppy disk icon, select its properties window and type in the new name.

LAN Acronym for Local Area Network. LANs are now commonplace in most businesses, allowing users to send email and share resources such as files, printers, modems, etc. Currently, larger companies are connection their LANs to the Internet, allowing users to connect to resources within or outside the LAN.

Language Windows 3.1 and 95 can support foreign languages. In most cases, the foreign country has a different set of accented characters and a different keyboard layout. The UK and USA use the QWERTY keyboard layout (this describes the first keys on the top left hand row). France uses the AZERTY layout. If you want to use a different language for display and printing you will have to change the language setup for the font used to support the accents and the keyboard layout for Windows. If you want to use central European or Asian languages, you'll need to buy new fonts.

Laptop A small computer that you can carry around. A laptop normally has a 'clam shell' construction with a fold-down lid that houses the screen, a keyboard (often slightly smaller than full-size) and a floppy and a hard disk drive. An internal battery pack provides power for a few hours. Most laptop PCs now provide color screens and as much computing power as a desktop, but with the convenience of being portable.

Laser Disc Large, metallic-looking records about the size of 33-RPM albums (12 inches in diameter), sometimes called videodiscs. Laserdiscs can store a vast amount of information in text, sound, and images. To play a laserdisc, you need a laserdisc player and either a computer monitor or television set. Laserdiscs come in two formats. CLV (constant linear velocity) is accessed by time and CAV (constant angular velocity) is accessed by frame number.

Laser Disc Player A self-contained unit approximately the size of a videocassette recorder (VCR) that plays laserdiscs. Typically used in education for movies or interactive multimedia courseware. Their primary advantage over VCRs as a video playback unit is their ability to provide quick random access to any location on the laserdisc within the seconds.

Laser Printer Printer that produces very high quality text and graphics using a laser beam. The beam draws the characters as tiny dots-normally 300 or 600 dots per inch-on to a special drum. The drum then attracts a fine black powder (called toner) to these dots which is transferred to a sheet of paper. The final stage is to heat the toner which melts it on the paper forming a permanent image. Laser printers are more expensive than almost any other type of printer, but are generally faster and excellent quality. Other types of printer include inkjet and dot-matrix.

LATA Local Access And Transport Areas.

Launch This is another way of saying that you are starting a program. You can launch a program by double-clicking on its icon within Windows or by typing in the program name at the DOS prompt.

Layer Group of neurons having connections to the same inputs and sending outputs to the same destinations.

Layer Diagram Network architecture figure showing the layers and the weight matrices connecting them. Each layer's transfer function is indicated with a symbol. Sizes of input, output, bias, and weight matrices are shown. Individual neurons and connections are not shown.

Layer Weights Weights connecting layers to other layers. Such weights need to have nonzero delays if they form a recurrent connection (i.e., a loop).

Lazy Swapper Programs reside on a swapping device, the backing store. When we want to execute a program, we swap it into memory. However, we use a "lazy" swapper. The lazy swapper never swaps a page into memory unless it is needed. There are many advantages to using a lazy swapper. It decreases the swap time and the amount of physical memory needed, allowing an increased degree of multiprogramming.

LBA (Logical Block Addressing) A technique for addressing data on a computer disk in which sector or numbered consecutively for identifying and retrieval.

LCD (Liquid Crystal Displays) Liquid crystal refers to the fact that these compounds have a crystalline arrangement of molecules. Flat panel display commonly use. Rematic thread like) liquid-crystal compounds that tend to keep the long axes of the rod shaped molecules aligned.

LCD is made up by placing thermo tropic liquid crystal material between two sheets of glass. A set of electrodes is attached to each sheet of glass. Horizontal electrodes are attached to one glass plate and vertical electrodes are fitted to other plate.

LCD Screen Portable computers do not have room for a bulky monitor. Instead, they often use LCD (Liquid Crystal Display) screen. There are three types of LCD screen available: monochrome, DSTN (Double Super Twisted Nematic) color and TFT (Thin Film Transistor) color. Monochrome screens have a thin light source behind the screen that glows. This is the cheapest type of LCD screen available for laptop PCs and provides a reasonable display. The two-color LCD screens are now a standard feature of laptops. DSTN screens are cheaper but do not have such good color as TFT screen. Color TFT screens are often brighter and sharper than monitors for desktop PCs.

Learning Process by which weights and biases are adjusted to achieve some desired network behavior.

Learning Rate Training parameter that controls the size of weight and bias changes during learning.

Learning Rule Method of deriving the next changes that might be made in a network *or* a procedure for modifying the weights and biases of a network.

Leased Line A dedicated, full-time connection used to link a user or network to an Internet Service Provider or another network.

LEC Local exchange carrier.

Left-Handed

If you are left-handed and are trying to use a mouse, you might find it tricky. The mouse is designed for right-handed people. However, many mice come with setup software that lets you swap the way the buttoned operate. You can use the Settings of Windows 95 to do the same.

Levenberg-Marquardt

Algorithm that trains a neural network 10 to 100 times faster than the usual gradient descent back propagation method. It always computes the approximate Hessian matrix, which has dimensions *n*-by-*n*.

Lexical Analysis

It is the first phase of a compiler. It is also called has scanning, scans a source program form left to right character by character and group them into tokens having a collective meaning. It performs 2 important tasks. First, it scans a source program character by character from left to right and groups them into token (or syntactic element). The second task performed during lexical analysis is to make entry of tokens into a symbol table if it is not there. Some other tasks performed during lexical analysis are:

To remove all comments, tabs, blank spaces and machine characters.

To produce error message occurred in a source program.

Life Cycle Of Java Applete

In Applet life cycle an Applet contains a set of default behavior from the Applet class. When the Applet is loaded, it runs through different states. The different states are Born or Initialization state, Running state, Idle state and Dead or destroyed state.

Line Search Function

Procedure for searching along a given search direction (line) to locate the minimum of the network performance.

L

Linear Hashing	**Linear hashing** is a dynamic hash table algorithm invented by Witold Litwin (1980), and later popularized by Paul Larson. Linear hashing allows for the expansion of the hash table one slot at a time. The frequent single slot expansion can very effectively control the length of the collision chain. The cost of hash table expansion is spread out across each hash table insertion operation, as opposed to being incurred all at once. Linear hashing is therefore well suited for interactive applications.
Linear Search	**Linear search** or **sequential search** is a method for finding a particular value in a list that consists of checking every one of its elements, one at a time and in sequence, until the desired one is found. Linear search is the simplest search algorithm; it is a special case of brute-force search. Its worst case cost is proportional to the number of elements in the list; and so is its expected cost, if all list elements are equally likely to be searched for. Therefore, if the list has more than a few elements, other methods (such as binary search or hashing) will be faster, but they also impose additional requirements.
Linear Transfer Function	Transfer function that produces its input as its output.
Link Distance	Number of links, or steps that must be taken to get to the neuron under consideration.
Linking Information	In windows ,you can link different types of data together using its OLE function .you can include a spreadsheet inside a document, which is then automatically updated whenever the spreadsheet change.
Listserv	An automatic mailing list distribution system. listserv exist for a multitude of professional, education, and special interest groups.

usually, you have to send an email to a list server with the subject SUBSCRIBE list name or something to that effect. You are then subscribed to that list and (depending on the service) will receive regular mail from a single source or from all members who send email to the list server. Listserv was originally designed for the Bitnet/EARN network.

Loader The loader or linker is a program that takes the Object file generated by the Assembler program and generates a file in binary code called the COM file or the EXE file. The COM (or EXE) file is the only executable file – i.e., the only file that can be executed by the microcomputer. To execute the program, the COM file is called under the control of the operating system and executed.

Local Minimum Minimum of a function over a limited range of input values. A local minimum might not be the global minimum.

Log Off To stop using a network and work individually. Your computer is still physically connected to the network, but you have told the network software that you do not want to use the network features or resources. Log off can apply either to a local area network or to an online system, such as CompuServe or MSN. In the case of the latter two, you log off and disconnect by hanging up the phone line to the online service.

Log On A command that tells the network you want to use the network resources. Normally you need to enter your user name and password, which is then verified by the network software before allowing you to access the resources.

L

Login Script A series of instructions that are automatically run when you log on to a network. For example, if you log on to your office network in the morning by typing your name and password, the login script might remind you of important information or just say good morning.

Logs The log, which is usually written to stable storage, contains the redundant data required to recover from volatile storage failures and also from errors discovered by the transaction or the database system.

Log-Sigmoid Transfer Function Squashing function of the form shown below that maps the input to the interval (0, 1).

$f(n) = 1/\ (1 + e^{-n})$

Long Filename A feature of windows that lets you gives files a long name (up to 254 characters). Before windows 95 was released, file names were limited to a maximum number of eight characters. For example, before windows 95, your letter would be called something like lett27.doc.

Loop A set of program instruction that is executed until a specific condition is met.

Loop Ender A value expressed in a loop instruction to signal a branch & prevent unnecessary iterations of the loop.

Loop Feedback The output values that modified input for the next iteration of a loop instruction.

Loosely Coupled Descriptive of computers that are connected, but are capable of independent operation.

Lost Files If you lose a file, or forget where you've stored it on your hard disk, use the find feature of windows 95 in the start button's menu.

Lower Bound Theory If f(n) is the time for some algorithm, then we write $f(n) = \Omega(g(n))$ to mean that g(n) is a lower bound for f(n). Formally this equation can be written if there exists positive constants C and n_0 such that $|f(n)| \geq C|g(n)|$ for $n > n_0$.

LSI (Large Scale Integration) The process of designing more than a thousand gates on a single chip. Similarly, the terms VLSI (Very large scale integration) and SLSI (Super large scale integration) are used to indicate the scale of integration.

Lurking Non-active participation on the part of a subscriber to a mailing list, a Usenet newsgroup, and IRC channel, a video connection, or any other internet communication devises. If you're "lurking", you're generally just listening to the discussion. It's usually best to lurk you're a beginner or if you are new to a communication group. This allows you to get up to speed on the history or acceptable behavior of the group.

M

Machine Language This is a sequence of instructions written in the form of binary numbers consisting of 1's, 0's to which the computer responds directly. An instruction prepared in any machine language will have at least two parts. The first part is the command or operation, which tells the computer what functions, is to be performed. All computers have an operation code for each of its functions. The second part of the instruction is the operand or it tells the computer where to find or store the data that has to be manipulated.

Macintosh Computers Macs computers manufactured by apple corporation. Most people agree that Macs are easy to use than IBM clone. People doing a lot of graphical work, such as desktop publishing, generally prefer Macintosh.

Macro A series of command or operations that can be run at any time. For example, if you always carry out a series of operations on your text to run it to a monthly report (perhaps, changing the font, adding a table, searching and replacing one character for another), then you could record a macro to do all these functions automatically. All most all world processor and spreadsheet programs can record and playback macros.

Mail In the world of computer networking, "mail" refers to electronic mail or e-mail.

Mail Merge To automatically include the address details from a database in a standard letter. If you want to tell your friends that you are moving house, write a standard letter include name and address fields from your database. Almost all word processor programs let you carry out a mail merge with an external database.

Mail Reflector A program that distributes files or information in response to send request via email. Many list serve have mail reflectors. You can request documents of a reflector by sending message with subject SEND document name or a similar command. Mail reflectors are also being used to provide FTP-lie services for users with limited internet access.

Mailing List A list of email addresses used to forward messages to group of people. When you subscribe to mailing list, you receive all mail sent to that list (see also list serve).

Mainframe, Minicomputer, Micro-Computer Three sizes of computers. Big corporation use mainframes and large school systems might use mid-range computers, sometimes called a minicomputer, as a file serve and administrative tool. The correct term for microcomputer is personal computer or pc.

Management Information System A company or origination's is facilitates for gathering, storing and managing data for using decision making.

Management Information Systems (Mis) Data abstracted from routine processing are further processed using well thought out rules to obtain tactical information. Such systems are called MIS.

Manhattan Distance The Manhattan distance between two vectors x and y is calculated as D = sum(abs(x-y))

Many To Many Mapping An entity in 'A' is associated with any number of entities in B, & an entity in B is associated with any number of entities in 'A'.

Many To One Mapping An entity in 'A' is associated with at most one entity in B. an entity in B, however, can be associated with any number of entities in 'A'.

Mapping Cardinalities Cardinality ratios, express the number of exits to which another entity can be associated via a relationship set.

M

Matrix Computation It includes numerical evaluation of determinations, the solution of simultaneous system of linear equations, the inversion of matrices, and determination of eigenvalues & eigenvectors of a matrix.

Maximize The command that increases the size of the window so that it fills the entire screen. To maximize a window, click on the maximize button-the up arrow at the very top right-hand corner of the window.

Maximum Performance Increase Maximum amount by which the performance is allowed to increase in one iteration of the variable learning rate training algorithm.

Maximum Step Size Maximum step size allowed during a linear search. The magnitude of the weight vector is not allowed to increase by more than this maximum step size in one iteration of a training algorithm.

Mb Or M-Byte Stands for megabyte. A measure of the data capacity of the storage device that is equal to 1,048,576 bytes (which is equal to the power of 20 or 220). Megabytes are used to measure the storage capacity of hard disk drives or many more (RAM).

Mccall's Quality Factor The factors that affect software quality can be categorized in to broad groups

1) Factors that can be directly measured (ex. Deflect per function point) &

2) Factors that can be measured only indirectly (ex. usability or maintainability).

McCall provides the following descriptions:

a) Correctness

b) Reliability

c) Efficiency

d) Integrity

e) Usability

f) Maintainability

g) Flexibility

h) Testability.

Mean Square Error Function Performance function that calculates the average squared error between the network outputs a and the target outputs t.

Media 1) Something that will store or carry information. It's vague term, but it generally refers to floppy disks or CDROM disks.

2) Information used in a multimedia presentation which could be sound, graphic or video.

Media Player A utility program supplied free with windows that allows you to control installed multimedia hardware including videodisks or audio CDs, or playback multimedia files including sound or video files.

Meg A slang term of megabyte.

Megabyte See Mb

Megahertz See MHz

Melding The Problem & The Process See in project planning.

Memory This means same device that can store information, but it's also used to refer to electronic components that can store data and are used to provide RAM in your PC. Electronic memory chips only remember data for as long as electricity is supplied. This is not same as disk storage, which is long-term data storage on magnetic media.

(1) Voltage memory i.e. erased when power is shut down; the area in a computer or printer where data is held during processing.

(2) Static memory such as on a hard or floppy disk; that part of a computer where programs & data are stored.

Memory Address Register MAR) It holds the address of the active memory location. It is loaded from the program control register when an instruction is read from memory.

Memory Buffer Register (MBR) It holds the contents of the memory word read from, or written in, memory. An instruction word placed in this register is transferred to the instruction register. A data word placed in this register is accessible for operation with the accumulator register or for transfer to the I/O register. A word to be stored in a memory location must first be transferred to the MBR, from where it is written in memory.

Memory Fragmentation A job which needs m words of memory may be run in a region of n words, where n ≥ m. The difference between these two numbers (n-m) is internal fragmentation, memory which is internal to a region, but is not being used. External fragmentation occurs when a region is unused and available, but too small or any waiting job. Both types of fragmentation are sources of memory waste in MFT. MFT-modified final judgment.

Menu A list of selectable network functions. A "main menu" usually leads to other command or options.

Merge Sort In computer science, **merge sort** (also commonly spelled **merge sort**) is an O(*n* log *n*) comparison-based sorting algorithm. Most implementations produce a stable sort, which means that the implementation preserves the input order of equal elements in the sorted output. Merge sort is a divide and conquer algorithm that was invented by John von Neumann in 1945.

Message Any message carried on the network, including conference topics and responses, and e-mail.

Message Box A small window that pops up on the screen to warn you of an event or condition or error. For example, if you try to save a document with the same name as an existing file, a message box pops up to ask if you want to change the filename or replace the existing file with the new one.

Message Communication In OOPS An object oriented program consists of a set of objects that communicate with each other. The process of programming in an object oriented language therefore, involves the following basic steps:

Creating classes that define objects and their behavior.

Creating objects from class definitions.

Establishing communication among objects.

Message Switching It is unlike circuit switching does not establish a dedicated path between two communicating devices. Instead each message is treated as an independent unit and includes its own destination and source addresses. Each complete message is then transmitted from device to device through the internetwork. Each intermediate device receivers the message, store it until the next device is ready to receive it and then forwards it to the next device. For this reason a message switching network is sometimes referred to as a store and forward network.

Metadata It is a data that describes other data.

MHEG It stands for Multimedia/Hypermedia Expert Group. This is a standard for hypermedia document representation. It is suited to interactive hypermedia applications and many interactive multimedia applications currently available, on CD-ROM. In MHEG, the users provide the data file formats, and it provides a hook to identify a variety of types. By supporting various file types it can provide a standardized interchange mechanism independent of file structure. MHEG objects come in four types: input (e.g. a button), output (e.g., a graphic), interactive (contains input and output) and hyper-object (input and output with links between). It supports various synchronization modes for presenting output objects.

MHz Stands for megahertz. A measure of the frequency of a timing signal that's equal to 1,000,000 cycles per second. The higher the number, the faster the clock that's generating the signal. This normally refers to the main clock that sets the timing signal for the processor chip in your PC. The faster the timing signal, the faster the processor will run.

Microcontroller A device that includes microprocessor, memory, and I/O signal lines on a single chip, fabricated using VLSI technology.

Microphone A device that converts sound waves into electrical signals. To record sound on your pc, you need a microphone to convert sound to electrical signals.

Microprocessor The microprocessor is a programmable integrated device that has computing and decision-making capability similar to that of the central processing unit.

A microprocessor is a multipurpose, programmable, clock-driven, register-based electronic device that reads binary instructions from a storage device called memory, accepts binary data as input and processes data according to those instructions, and provides results as output.

A semiconductor device (integrated circuit) manufactured by using the LSI technique. It includes the ALU, register arrays, and control circuits on a single chip.

Microprocessors Main computer chip that provides speed and capabilities of the computer, also called CPU.

Micro-Programmed Control Unit The sequence of execution of micro-operations happens through a program? Such a program will consist of instructions, with each of the instruction describing:

One or more micro-operations to be executed and

The information aborts the micro-instruction to be executed next.

Such an instruction is termed as micro-instruction and such a program is termed as a micro-program or firmware.

MID File extensions for data conforming to the protocol for interaction between digitized musical instruments & a computer.

MIDI Stands for musical instruments digital interface. A special interface that lets your computer control musical instruments, such as a synthesizer, keyboard 0r drum machine. To create a MIDI interface for your PC-, which is often part of a sound card and a cable that runs to your musical instrument?

MIDI Adapter Hardware that provides communities between a computer & a sound device.

MIDI Compatible Sound Devices An instrument such as a keyboard or synthesizer that can be used to record & play back sound through a computer.

M

MIDI File

File stored on your PC that contains musical notes and sound information that can be sent via a MIDI interface card to musical instrument. Midi file can also contain information that describes the type of sound played as well as the note. For example, to inform the synthesizer to sounds like a piano or trumpet.

MIDI Mapper

Program that's supplied with windows 3.1x and that allows experienced MIDI users to change the way in which musical notes are sent to each instrument that's connected to the PC. For example, you could see the MIDI mapper to redirect all the notes meant for the drum machine to the electronic piano.

Minimize

To shrink an application window down to an icon. To do this, select the down-arrow button in the top right-hand corner of the window. Minimizing an application allows you to run several applications allows you to run several applications at the same time, minimizing the once which you're not using. In windows 3.1x the minimized applications as an icon in the bottom left-hand corner of the screen. To go back to the application, double-click on the minimized icon. In windows 95, the application shrinks down to an icon on the status bar; you can switch back to the application with a single click on the icon.

Mirror Site

Due to the popularity of some FTP and web sites came into existence. They are areas on a computer that "mirror" or contain an exact replica of the directory structure of another computer. If you have trouble getting connected to an FTP site, for example, because of the high amount of traffic, you can usually connect to a mirror site that contains the same information on a different computer. Mirror sites are usually updated once a day.

Mnemonic Keyboard Shortcut A special key sequence that is a shortcut to a menu option or function in an application. For example, pressing the Alt and F4 (written Alt-F4) keys at the same time will exit an application. Similarly, Ctrl and S (Ctrl-S) will save your current document in Microsoft applications.

MNP Microcom network protocol. Error-checking and compression routines that make modems communicate faster and more reliably.

Modem A devise that converts electronic signals from your PC into sound signals that can be transmitted over a phone line. To receive information the modem works in reverse and converts the sound signals back into digital electronic signals. Modems are used to connect to the internet or to an online service, such as CompuServe. Some modems are internal and you have to open your PC and fit the modem into a free expansion slot. Most modems are external and plug into the serial port of your PC. Current modems can transfer data at 28,800 bits per second (bps), which is roughly equivalent to one and a half pages of A4 text a second. If you are buying a modem, make sure it has error detection and correction functions called V numbers. You might find it useful to buy a modem that can work as a fax to send and receive text and images to other fax machines.

Modem Setup Modem speed or baud rate, parity, data bits, stop bits, and duplex must be set the same at the user's computer as at the network system. Communication software is used to set up the modem.

Modularity The functional independence of program components.

M

MOI Model of Leadership	(1) Motivation:-The ability to converge (by "push or pull") technical people to produce to their best ability. (2) Organization: - The ability to mold existing process (or invent new ones) that will enable the initial concept to be translated into a final product. (3) Ideas or innovation: - The ability to encourage people to create & feel creative even when they must work within bounds established for a particular s/w product or application.
Momentum	Technique often used to make it less likely for a back-propagation network to get caught in a shallow minimum.
Momentum Constant	Training parameter that controls how much momentum is used.
Monitor	Device that displays the text and graphics from your PC. It looks and works rather like a TV set. Images are displayed as tiny dots on the screen (the smaller and closer the dots, the sharper the image). If you do a lot of design or DTP, you might consider a screen that's bigger than the usual 15 inch mirror. The size is measured across the longest diagonal.
Monitor Program	A program that interprets the input from a keyboard and converts the input into its binary equivalent.
Monochrome Monitor	A monitor that can only displays black, white and grey text and images.
Morphing	Special effect used in multimedia and games in which one image gradually turns into another. For example, a tiger might gradually turn into a bucket over a few seconds.

Mosaic A graphical browser for the World Wide Web that supports hypermedia. The NCSA (National Super Computer Association) invented the Mosaic browser, which quickly became the industry standard. Netscape Communications Corporation later invented the Netscape Navigator, which has redefined the content on the Web. Other major companies entered the browser market with little success, until Microsoft launched their Internet Explorer which now contends with Navigator as the browser of choice .the term mosaic is sometimes used in correctly as a synonym for the *world wide web.*

Mosaic A graphical browser for the world web that supports hypermedia. The NCSA (National Super Computer Association) invented the mosaic browser, which quickly became the industry standard. Netscape communications corporation later invented the Netscape navigator, which has redefined the content on the web. Other major companies entered the browser market with little success, until Microsoft launched their internet explorer which now condenses with Navigator as the browser of choice. The term Mosaic is sometimes used incorrectly as a synonym for the World Wide Web.

MOTHER BOARD The main circuit board in your computer. If you open the computer you'll see the mother board as the case. It is normally varnished green project the tiny connections and has the main *electronic component and connectors soldered on it.*

M

MOUSE Small hand held device that's moved on a flat surface to control the position of the pointer on a screen. A mouse normally has 2 buttons. In windows, the left hand button select text or selects an application. The right hand button selects option for the item. If you want to change a file so that it can only be read, and not written to, read the file with a single click on left hand button. Now click once on right hand button to display properties for this file.

MOVE FILE A file stored on disk that contains a series of image that make up an animation or a video clip.

MOVIE PLAYER A program supplied with windows that allow you to play back and edit movie files.

MPC Stands for multimedia pc. A set of minimum requirements for a pc that will allow you to run most multimedia software. Generally will refer to PCs that have 4mb or more of RAM a 486SX processor or better at least a 160mb hard disk a CD-ROM XA drive ,16-bit sound card and MIDI port.

***MPEG* (Motion Picture Experts Group)** The main algorithm used to compress videos and have been internationals standards since 1993. Because movies contain both images and sounds, MPEG can compress both audio and video since video takes up more bandwidth and also contains more redundancy than audio.

MS-DOS Software that controls and coordinates the basic function of a computer. If you are running windows, the functions of MS-DOS have been integrated on windows if you are using windows or do not have windows then you are relying on MS-DOS to control computer.

MSI (Medium Scale Integration) The process of designing more than a hundred gates on a single chip.

Mu Parameter Initial value for the scalar.

Multilevel Queue Scheduling The multilevel queue scheduling partition the processes into different groups. For example: System process, user Interactive process, Batch process, and System Maintenance process.

Multi-List File Organization A multi-list is really only a slightly modified inverted file. There is one list per keyword, i.e. $h_i = 1$. The records containing a particular keyword K_i are chained together to form the K_i-list and the start of the K_i-list are given in the directory. Since there is no K_3-list, the field reserved for its pointer could well have been omitted. So could any blank pointer field, so long as no ambiguity arises as to which pointer belongs to which keyword. One way of ensuring this, particularly if the data values (attribute-values) are fixed format, is to have the pointer not pointing to thc bcginning of the record but pointing to the location of the next pointer in the chain. The multi-list is designed to overcome the difficulties of updating an inverted file. The addresses in the directory of an inverted file are normally kept in record-number order. But, when the time comes to add a new record to the file, this sequence must be maintained, and inserting the new address can be expensive. No such problem arises with the multi-list; we update the appropriate K-lists by simply chaining in the new record. The penalty we pay for this is of course the increase in search time. This is in fact typical of many of the file structures. Inherent in their design is a trade-off between search time and update time.

M

MULTIMEDIA	The delivery of information using 2 or more formats including text, graphics , audio still images music, animation, and motion videos .today, the term implies "interactive multimedia" in which these various types of info are presented interactively by a computer in response to user input.
Multimedia	It is the term for different media like graphics, animation, sound and video all wrapped in one interactive package. The basic idea is to manage and co-ordinate the various devices of communication and entertainment electronics with the PC as a central controller. Multimedia brings dazzle to presentations, actions to games, fun to learning and communication system.
Multiple Inheritance	It permits a class to have more than one super class and to inherit features from all parents. This permits mixing of information from two or more sources. This is a more complicated form of generalization than single inheritance, which restricts the class hierarchy to a tree.
MULTIPLEXED	A system that manages signals between two or more devices simultaneously.
Multiplexer	It allows sharing of a common line by more than one input lines. It connects multiple input lines to a single output line. At a specific time one of the input lines is selected and the selected input is passed on to the output line.
Multiprocessing Operating System	It manage the operation of computer system that incorporate multiple processors. Multi processors are multitasking system by definition because they support simultaneously execution of multi tasks on different processors. Depending on implementation, multitasking may or may not be allowed on individual processors. Except

management and scheduling of multiple processors, multiprocessor O.S. provide the usual complement of other system services that may quality them as time-sharing, real time, or a combination of operating system.

Multiprogramming It is an attempt to increase CPU utilization by always having something for the CPU to execute.

Multiprogramming It is essentially multiplexing of system resources such as processors, memory and I/O devices among a number of active programs. Potential benefits of concurrent execution of programs include increased performance, resource utilization and responsiveness of a computer system.

Multitasking On the multitasking Operating System number of programs runs simultaneously on a single processor without necessarily supporting elaborate forms of memory management and file management.

MULTI-TASKING The ability of windows to run several programs at once. The trick is that the windows switch very rapidly between the tasks giving you the impression that they are running in parallel.

MULTI-USER SYSTEM The computer system design to managed input and output from several terminals at same time.

MY COMPUTER ICON Normally at the top left of the screen on a pc running windows. It contains an over view of a PC. If you double click on it you will see the peripherals linked to that system.

N

NAME	The description given to a file, folder, pointer or pc on a network. If you want to change the name of the folder in windows move the pointer over the name and click once wait a couple of seconds and you will be able to type a new name.
National Informatics Center Network (Nicnet)	In order to provide IT help to the government and Public Sector Undertakings, this project was set up in 1980. It connects various government (INDIAN) departments together through its network. The main objective of NICNET is to extend network and communication infrastructure to the government departments for storage of data and its exchange within the government departments.
Natural Language	An approach to speech application design that encourages users to speak naturally to the system. Contrast with directed dialogue.
Natural Merge Sort	A natural merge sort is similar to a bottom up merge sort except that any naturally occurring runs (sorted sequences) in the input are exploited. In the bottom up merge sort, the starting point assumes each run is one item long. In practice, random input data will have many short runs that just happen to be sorted. In the typical case, the natural merge sort may not need as many passes because there are fewer runs to merge. In the best case, the input is already sorted (i.e., is one run), so the natural merge sort need only make one pass through the data.
Neighborhood	Group of neurons within a specified distance of a particular neuron. The neighborhood is specified by the indices for all the neurons that lie within a radius d of the winning neuron i^*.

Net Input Vector Combination, in a layer, of all the layer's weighted input vectors with its bias.

Netiquette The combination of the words Net and etiquette, this refers to the proper behavior on a network, and more generally the Internet. The key element in Netiquette is conditions to achieve an acceptable ratio while others are able to sort out background noise and compensate for copy i.e., Scanned in at angles or that contains broken letters caused by poor copy or a bad scan the most sophisticated program are capable of learning and recording corrections made by the user and compensating on future reads.

Network A collection of two or more computer interconnected by telephone lines, coaxial cables, satellite links, radio, and/or some other communication technique. A computer "network" is a group of computers which are connected together and which communicate with one another for a common purpose. Computer networks support "people and organization" networks, users who also share a common purpose for communicating.

Network A collection of two or more computers interconnected by, telephone lines, coaxial cables, satellite links, radio, and/or some other communication technique. A computer "network" is a group of computers which are connected together and which communicate with one another for a common purpose. Computer networks support "people and organization" networks, users who also a share a common purpose for communicating.

Network Data Model The data in network model are represented by collection of records and relationships among data are represented by links which can be viewed as pointers. The records in the data base are organized as collections of arbitrary graphs. In a network database, the collection of records is connected to one another by means of links. A record is a collection of fields, each of which contains only one data value.

Network Drive A disk drive you can access, but that is physically located on another PC on the network. To Windows, it appears to be just another disk drive.

Network Drive A disk drive you can access, but that is physically located on another PC on the network. To windows, it appears to be just another disk drive.

Network Neighborhood (Nn) An icon that appears on the Windows Desktop if you are connected to a network. If you double-click on NN, you'll see all the other PCs linked to the network and can share files.

Network Neighborhood (Nn) An icon that appears on the windows desktop if you are connected to a network. If you double click on NN, you'll see all the other PCs linked to the network and can share files.

Network News Transfer Protocol (Nntp) An industry standard protocol for the distribution, inquiry, retrieval, and posting of news articles.

Network News Transfer Protocol (Nntp) An industry standard protocol for the distribution, inquiry, retrieval, and posting of news articles.

Network Printer A printer connected to a PC connected to a network. Letting you to use the printer as if it were connected to your PC.

Network Printer A printer connected to a PC connected to a network. Letting you to use the printer as if it were connected to your PC.

Network Server A special dedicated computer used to support large office networks and store files.

Network Server A special dedicated computer used to support large office networks and store files.

Neuron Basic processing element of a neural network. Includes weights and bias, a summing junction, and an output transfer function. Artificial neurons, such as those simulated and trained with this toolbox, are abstractions of biological neurons.

Newsgroups Electronic bulletin boards on the Internet that specialize on particular topics, such as nursing, aviation, football, gardening, piano tuning, and many aspects of computers. There are over 25,000 newsgroups. In order to access newsgroups, you must have software known as a "newsreader" (most web browsers act as newsreaders). You also must have access to a "news server", through which you access the newsgroups.

Newsgroups Electronic bulletin boards on the Internet that specialize on particular topics, such as nursing, football, gardening, piano tuning, and many aspects of computers. There are over 25,000 newsgroups. In order to access newsgroups, you must have software known as a "newsreader" (most web browser act as newsreaders). You also must have access to a "news server", through which you access the newsgroups.

NFA Non deterministic finite acceptors. Non determinism means a choice of moves for an automaton. Rather than prescribing a unique move in each situation, we allow a set of possible moves. Formally, We achieve this by defining the transition function so that its range is A set of possible states.

N

Nibble	The term nibble, which stands for a group of four bits. A byte has two nibbles.
NIC (Network Interface Card)	A PC card that provides connection to a computer network.
NIST	National Institute of Standards and Technology.
Node	A central computer in a computer network; also called a Host or Server.
Node	A central computer in a computer network; also called a "host" or "server".
Noise	Unwanted random signal that sounds like hiss on a record.
Non-Deterministic Algorithm	Defined as algorithm to contain operations whose outcome is not uniquely defined but is limited to a specified set of possibilities. The machine executing such operations is allowed to choose any one of these outcomes subject to termination condition to be defined later. The time required by a non-deterministic algorithm performing on any given input is the minimum number of steps needed to reach a successful completion. If there exists a sequence of choices leading to such a completion.
Non-Preemptive Scheduling	In batch, non-preemption scheduling implies that, once scheduled, a selected jobs runs to completion. In other words, the running process is not forced to relinquish ownership of the processor when higher priority processes become ready for execution. However, when the running process becomes suspended as a result of its own action, say, by waiting for an I/O completion, another ready process may be scheduled.
Nonprocedural DML	Require a user to specify what data are needed without specifying how to get those data.

Non-Relocatable Programs

A Non-relocatable programs is one which cannot be made to execute in any area of storage other than the one designated for it at the time of its coding or translation. Non-relocatability is the result of address sensitivity of code and lack of information regarding:

Which parts of the program are address sensitive and

In what manner.

Normalization

It is the processes of transformation of the conceptual schema (logical data structures) of the database into a computer represent able form. Normalization is the process of removing the redundancies from incoming data. Normalization is a technique to which helps the user to group the data and place the data in a table.

Normalization is a process which ensures the inconsistencies are not introduced into the database.

Novell Netware

The most popular network system in the PC world Is Novell NetWare. It was designed to be used by companies Downsizing from a mainframe to a network of PC's. In such systems, each user has a desktop PC functioning as a client. In addition, some Number of powerful PC's operates as servers, providing file service, Database service & other services to a collection of clients. In other Words Novell NetWare is based on the client-server model.

NP-Complete

A problem that is NP-complete has the property that it can be solved in polynomial time if and only if all other NP- complete problems can also be solved in polynomial time.

N

NP-Completeness The distinction between problems that can be solved by a polynomial time algorithm and problems for which no polynomial time algorithm is known. It is an unexplained phenomenon that for many of the problems we know and study. The best algorithms for their solutions have computing times that cluster into two groups. The first group consists of problems whose solution times are bounded by polynomials of small degree. The theory of NP completeness which we present here does not provide a method of obtaining polynomial time algorithms for problems in the second group. Nor does it say that algorithms of this complexity do not exist. Instead, what we do is show that many of the problems for which there are no known polynomials time algorithms are computationally related. In fact, we establish two classes of problems. These are given the names NP-Hard and NP-Complete.

NP-Hard If an NP-hard problem can be solved in polynomial time, then all NP-complete problems can be solved in polynomial time. All NP-complete problems are KP-hard but, some NP-hard problems are not known to be NP-complete.

Null Modem Cable Special cable that you link two PCs via their serial ports so they can exchange files.

Num-Lock Key Key at the top left of the numeric keypad that switches the keypad between cursor control and number entry.

O

Object	Anything on a PC screen. For example, a folder is an object, as is a section of text, graphics, part of spreadsheet, and even, in some cases, users and printers are objects.
Object	Object is an entity that can store, send and receive messages and an instance of a class. Each object contains both data and code to manipulate the data Objects can interact without having to know details of each object's data and code.
Object Based Logical Models	Used in describing data at the logical and view levels. They re-characterized by the fact that they provide fairly flexible structuring capabilities and allow data constraints to be specified explicitly.
Object Linking And Embedding (OLE)	System that lets you cut and paste data from one application to another, retaining the formatting and controls. You can select part of a spreadsheet, switch to a word processor and paste it into insert other objects, select Edit/Paste special and you will see a list of the types of object that you can include.
Object-Based Logical Models	Used in describing data at the logical & view levels. They are characterized by the fact that they provide fairly flexible structuring capabilities & allow data constrains to be specified explicitly.
OCR Program	A computer program that is intended to translategraphicsimagesofletters and numbers to character bits that can manipulated by a word processor, spreadsheet, or other similar program. The quality of such program varies greatly-some programs require near-perfect conditions to achieve an acceptable hit ratio while other are able to sort out background

noise and compensate for copy that is scanned in at angle or that contains broken letters caused by poor copy or a bad scan. The most sophisticated program is capable of learning by recording corrections made by the user and compensating on future reads.

ODA (Open Document Architecture) It is a document interchange format for transferring documents between open systems. It supports text and graphics, and an interface to MHEG is planned. Unlike SGML, ODA does concern itself with the physical appearance of the document.

OFFLINE Not connected to a network you can save money for pay of use networks by preparing your message offline by using your word processing software and uploading them instead of typing them in while you have connected the network.

Off-Line Operation The card readers & line printers were operated Off-line not by the main computer. The real gain in off-line Operations comes from the possibility of using multiple recorder-to-tape & tape-to-printer system for one CPU.

OIS Office information systems- office automation includes workstation based tools for document creation & document retrieval, tools for maintaining appointment calendars, & soon. An OIS database must allow queries pertaining to schedules, documents, & contents of documents.

OIS (Office Information System) Office Automation includes work station based tools for document creation and document retrieval, tools for maintaining appointment calendars, and soon. An OIS database must allow queries pertaining to schedules, documents, and contents of documents.

OLAP (Online Analytical Processing) It is used to analyze historical data and slice the business information required. OLAPs are often used by marketing managers. Slice of data that are useful to marketing managers can be – How many customers between the ages 24-25, that live in New Delhi, buy over rupees 2500/- worth of groceries a month?

OLE (Object Linking And Embedding) Object linking and embedding is a specification that allows users to integrate information from different applications. The most familiar features of OLE is to share data and present information in a single, compound document.

Omega Notation – Ω f(n) = Ω [g(n)], (read as "f of n equals omega of g(n)) iff there exist positive constants C and n_0 such that for all n> n_0 , $|f(n)| \geq C[g(n)]$

OMT Object Modeling Technique

OMT Object modeling technique.

One To Many Mapping An entity in 'A' is associated with any number of entities in 'B'. An entity in 'B', however, can be associated with at most one entity in 'A'.

One To Many Mapping An entity in 'A' is associated with any numbers of entities in 'B', an entity in 'B', however, can be associated with at most one entity in 'A'.

One To One Mapping An entity in 'A' is associated with at most one entity in 'B', and an entity in 'B' is associated with at most one entity in 'A'.

One To One Mapping An entity in "A" is associated with at most one entity in "B", & an entity in 'B', is associated with at most one entity in 'A'.

ONLINE *1.* A modem that is connected to another modem via a telephone line that is currently transferring info 2. A printer that is ready and ready to print. 3 connected to a network or via a network. Ex: send me a message online. In other words send me an e-mail message.

O

ONLINE HELP	help screen about a particular function of a program that is displayed within the program.
On-Line Transaction Processing (OLTP)	The method of processing data in which transactions are processed by a computer as and when they arise is called OLTP.
ONLINE-SYSTEM	A computer system in which data from an input device is fed directly into a main computer and processed immediately or at regular intervals a bar code scanner for ex: that record a scale at the stores cash register may also be connected to the stores computer in order to update inventory and scales report.
OOP'S (Object Oriented Programming)	The object oriented approach views a problem in terms of object involved rather than procedure for doing it. Object oriented programming is defined as a method of implementation in which programs organized are cooperative collections of objects, each of which is an instance of some class. The general concepts of OOPs are: Object, Class, Data Abstraction, Data Encapsulation, Inheritance, Polymorphism, Dynamic Binding, and Message Passing.
OOSE	Object Oriented Software Engineering
OOSE	Object oriented software engineering.
OPEN	1. To access a file and read its content using an application. Most windows application will read a file via the file/open menu option 2.to look inside a folder to view the list of files or sub folders stored in it pen a folder with a double click.
OPERABILITY	the ease of operation of a program.
OPERATING SYSTEM	the software that controls the action of different parts of pc in older PCs the operating system is called MS-DOS in modern PCs it is windows 95 that manages the screen keyboard disks and printers .

Operating System (O.S) Is a program which acts as an interface between a user of a computer & the computer hardware? Primary goal of the O.S is to make the computer system convenient to use and to use the computer Hardware in an efficient manner.

Operational Information It is used for day-to-day management of organizations. It is obtained by simple processing of data; it is well structured, and more voluminous.

OPERATOR a symbol that defines a mathematical function. X is the multiplication operator.

Optional Replacement An optional page replacement algorithm has The lowest page fault of all algorithms. An optional algorithm would Never suffer from be lady's anomaly. It states simply "Replace that page which will not be used for the longest period of time".

Ordering Phase Period of training during which neuron weights are expected to order themselves in the input space consistent with the associated neuron positions.

Oscillating Sort **Oscillating merge sort** or **oscillating sort** is a variation of merge sort used with tape drives that can read backwards. Instead of doing a complete distribution as is done in a tape merge, the distribution of the input and the merging of runs are interspersed. The oscillating merge sort does not waste rewind time or have tape drives sit idle as in the conventional tape merge.

OSI Reference Model Open systems interconnection reference model Because it deals with connecting open systems that is, systems that are open for communication with other systems.

OUTPUT Anything that is produced by your pc.

O

Output Layer	Layer whose output is passed to the world outside the network.
Output Vector	Output of a neural network. Each element of the output vector is the output of a neuron.
Output Weight Vector	Column vector of weights coming from a neuron or input.
Outstar Learning Rule	Learning rule that trains a neurons (or inputs) output weight vector to take on the values of the current output vector of the post weight layer. Changes in the weights are proportional to the neuron's output.
Over Fitting	Case in which the error on the training set is driven to a very small value, but when new data is presented to the network, the error is large.

P

PACKET	A bundle of data. On the internet data is broken into small chunks called packets that each traverses the network independently.
Packet Switching	Messages are broken up into packets, each of which includes a header with source, destination and intermediate node address information. Individual packets don't follow the same route; this is called independent routing.
PAGE DOWN KEY	key that moves down one page in word processor.
Page Fault	If we guess wrong, however and the program tries to access a page which was not brought into memory, then a page fault will occur.
PAGE PREVIEW	function in a word processor or other application that leds you lead the way the page will look b4 you printed.
PAGE SETUP	Option in an application that let you defines the margins paper orientation and paper size for the document.
Paging	It permits a programs memory to be noncontiguous, thus allowing a program to be allocated physical memory, wherever it is available.
Paging	It is a memory management scheme which removes the requirement of contiguous allocation of physical memory. Address mapping is used to maintain the illusion of contiguity of the virtual address space of a process despite its discontinuous placement in physical memory. Basically the physical memory is conceptually divided into a number of fixed size slots, called page frames. The virtual address space of a process is also split into fixed size blocks of the same size, called pages.

P

PALMTOP	Tiny computers that contain keyboard screen and storage.
PARALLEL PORT	Socket at the back of the pc that lets you connect in to a printer it sends data to the printer over eight parallel wires.
PARAMETER	a setting for a modern or a communication software.
PARENT FOLDER	a folder that contains other sub folder.
PARITY	a setting of a terminal or modern related to the type of error corrections system used when connected to a network.
PARSING	Explaining a sentence through a grammatical is familiar to most of us form a study of natural language and is called parsing. It is a way of describing sentence structure.
PARTITION	A way of dividing hard disk into chunks that can be addressed by separate disk drive letters. If you buy a large 1000GB hard disk you might find convenient to split into four 200 GB partitions called C: D: E: and F:
PARTITION TESTING	See black box testing.
Pass	Each traverse through all the training input and target vectors.
PASSWORD	A secret word or phrase that is associated with your user name and confirms your identity if you subscribe to an online service such as CompuServe you will have a public user name and number and a secret password that only you know.
PASSWORD AUTHENTICATION PROTOCOL (PAP)	one of the authentication methods that can be used when connecting to an ISP .PAP allows you to log in automatically without having to use an terminal window to type in your user name and password. One warning about PAP passwords are sent over the connection in text

format which means there is no protection if some is "listening in" on your connection.

PAT process activation table.

Pattern A vector.

Pattern Association Task performed by a network trained to respond with the correct output vector for each input vector presented.

Pattern Matching In computer science, pattern matching is the act of checking a perceived sequence of tokens for the presence of the constituents of some pattern. In contrast to pattern recognition, the match usually has to be exact. The patterns generally have the form of either sequences or tree structure. Uses of pattern matching include outputting the locations (if any) of a pattern within a token sequence, to output some component of the matched pattern, and to substitute the matching pattern with some other token sequence (i.e., search and replace).

Pattern Recognition Task performed by a network trained to respond when an input vector close to a learned vector is presented. The network "recognizes" the input as one of the original target vectors.

PC Stands for personal computer normally refers to an IBM compatible computer that uses an Intel processor originally the term refer to an IBM pc that used an 8088 processor with 512kb or 940kb of memory things have moved on and it is any computer that runs MS-DOS or windows.

PCX FILE Method of storing a graphic image file the standard is widely used and is a good way of moving graphic files between paint programs.

PDU Protocol Data Unit.

P

PENTIUM	A processor developed by Intel and used in high performance PCs it replaced the 80486 and is compatible with all the order 80 x 86 processor ranges.
Perceptron	Single-layer network with a hard-limit transfer function. This network is often trained with the perceptron learning rule.
Perceptron Learning Rule	Learning rule for training single-layer hard-limit networks. It is guaranteed to result in a perfectly functioning network in finite time, given that the network is capable of doing so.
Performance	As the algorithm becomes more complex, the time required to map a logical address to a physical address increases. For the simple systems, we need only compare or add to the logical address, operations that are quite fast. Paging and Segmentation can be as fast if the table is complimented in fast registers. A set of associative registers can reduce the performance degradation to an acceptable level.
Performance	Behavior of a network.
PERFORMANCE	It is measured by processing speed response time resource consumption through put efficiency.
PERIPHERAL	Anything extra or added on for your computer such as a modem a mouse or a fax adapter. It can be added on externally or installed inside the machine.
PERSONAL COMPUTER	The name is usually applied to IBM compatible microcomputers which use the Intel family of microprocessor and in particular run MS-DOS or windows IBM produced the first pc in early 80s other main type of pc found in schools are APPLE and ACORN.

PERT Graph — The **Program** (or **Project**) **Evaluation and Review Technique**, commonly abbreviated **PERT**, is a statistical tool, used in project management, that is designed to analyze and represent the tasks involved in completing a given project. First developed by the United States Navy in the 1950s, it is commonly used in conjunction with the critical path method (**CPM**).

Petri Net Models — It has four basic elements, they are places, and transitions, arcs, and tokens use to detect protocol failures in a way similar to the use of finite state machines.

PHIGS — Programmer's Hierarchical Interactive Graphics Standard.

Phoneme — The basic unit of sound. In the same way that written words are composed of letters, a spoken word is composed of various phonemes, though they may not line up precisely. For instance, the English word "food" has three phonemes (the "f" sound, the "oo" sound, and the "d" sound) but four letters. A speech engine uses its dictionary to break up vocabulary words and utterances into phonemes, and compares them to one another to perform speech recognition.

PHOTO CD — A standard of storing mm photos in digital format on a CD-ROM a photo CD is normally created at same time as the photo graphic film is created by digitalizing each frame at a resolution of 2048*3072 pixels with 24-bits color. One photo cd can hold 100 photographs. To read photo CD disc the CD rom drive should confirm to the CD-ROM XA standard. If all images are recorded on the photo CD at the same time then the disc can be read by the same session if further images are recorded at the same date then disc can only be read by multi session CD ROM drive.

PHOTOREALISTIC The computer image that has almost the same quality and clarity as a photograph. Images on photo CDs are photo realistic since they are scanned at resolution of 2048*3072 pixels in24 –bit color.

PHOTOTYPESETTER A device that can produce very high resolution text on photosensitive paper or film. The phototypesetter rather like a large laser printer normally uses the postscript page description language and can generate type at 2540 dpi. If the device capable of outputting text and half tone image, it is normally called an image setter. If you want to set a professional new looking settler or brochure you should send a disc of the file to a bureau that has a phototypesetter machine the bureau will produce a printed version that you can then give to a printer.

PHYSICAL DATA MODELS Used to describe data at lowest level in contrast to logical data models there are few physical data models in use 2 of the widely known once are unifying models &frame memory model.

PICA 1. Measurement equal to 12 points (0.166inch).

2. width of character in a type face usually 12 character per inch.

PIGEONHOLE PRINCIPLE if we put 'n' object in 'm' foxes if n>m then at least one box must have more than one tem in it this is such an obvious fact that it is surprising how many deep result can be obtained from it.

***PING* (Packet Internet Gopher)** The simplest way to test or type the response of an internet connection. A ping sends a request to an internet host and waits for a reply called a PONG when you PING an address you get a response telling you the number of seconds that took to make the connections. PING clients exist for a no of platforms or you can use a UNIX or windows prompt to issue a PING command directly.

PIRATING some people give to their family and software they have purchased ,so the other people won't have to pay for it this practice of giving commercial software is known as PIRATES when you buy a software program you do not own the program you only own a license to use the program. The program is owned by the company that developed it thus giving the program to others is stealing instead of being called pirates these people should be called thieves!

PIXEL The smallest single unit or point on a display or a printer whose color or brightness that can be controlled. A monitor that normally has a resolution of 72 pixels per inch whereas a laser printer has resolution of 300to 600 pixels per inch.

PLAY BACK to run a multimedia title or view a video clip or listen to recorded sound.

PLAYBACK HEAD An electronic device that reads the signals recorded on a storage medium and usually converts them to an electrical signal.

PLAYERS The software process is populated by players who can be categorized into one of 5 constituencies.

SENIOR MANAGERS who define the business issue that often have significance influence on the project.

MANEGER who must plan motivate organize, control the practitioners who do s/w work.

PRACTIONERS who deliver the technical skills that are necessary to engineer a product or application.

CUSTOMERS who specifies the requirements s/w to be engineered.

END USERS who interact with s/w once it is released for production use.

PLUG AND PLAY A development that is combination of hardware and software. The way it works is complex but the result is simple when you plug a new adapter card or a new disc controller network adapter or graphics adapter into your computer you don't have to configure it or set any switches. when you next switch on your computer and run windows it will automatically configure and set up the new adapter for you. This work with windows 95 and adapters that confirm to the plug and play standard.

PNG (Portable Network Graphics) It is an alternative to GIF. It provides a portable, legally free, well compress, well specified standard for bitmapped images files, which retain their high resolution.

Point-To-Point Networks It consist of many connections between individual pairs of machines. To go from the source to the destination, pocket on this type of network may have to first visit one or more intermediate machines. Often multiple routes of different lengths are possible, so routing algorithms play an important role in point-to-point networks.

Polak-Ribiére Update Method for computing a set of conjugate directions. These directions are used as search directions as part of a conjugate gradient optimization procedure.

Polymorphism It is a process of defining a number of objects of different classes into a group and call the member functions to carry out the operation of the objects using different functions. Polymorphism means the ability to take more than one form.

POP UP WINDOW A Window that can be displayed on the screen at any time on top of anything that is already on the screen. When the window is removed, the original screen display is restored. These are most often used to display warning messages or to confirm a choice. For example, if you try to save a file with a name that is the same as the existing file, you'll see a pop-up window that asks if you want to overwrite the existing file or change the name. These pop-up windows are often called dialogue boxes.

***POP*(Post Office Protocol)** A protocol designed to allow single users to read mail from a server there are 3 versions: POP, POP2, and POP3, when email is sent to you it is stored on the server until accessed by you. once you are authenticated the POP is used to transmit the stored email from the server to your local mail box on your client machine.

POP-UP MENU A menu that can be displayed on the screen at any time by pressing the appropriate key usually displayed on the material already on the screen once you have made a choice from the menu it disappears and original screen is restored.

PORT The plug to enable interface from computer to other pieces of hardware, via a cable. also used as a verb, "to port" meaning to move a film from one computer system network or conference to another.

P

Positive Linear Transfer Function — Transfer function that produces an output of zero for negative inputs and an output equal to the input for positive inputs.

Post Processing — Converts normalized outputs back into the same units that were used for the original targets.

POSTING — The act of placing a message in an online conference. the noun "posting" is sometimes complex or demanding application.

POTABLE HARD DISC — a hard disc &its drive that are connected to a computer though not mounted in the cabinet & that can be removed & attached to another computer that is set up with the proper connections that software.

Powell-Beale Restarts — Method for computing a set of conjugate directions. These directions are used as search directions as part of a conjugate gradient optimization procedure. This procedure also periodically resets the search direction to the negative of the gradient.

POWER USER — A user who needs the latest, fastest model of computer because she or he runs complex or demanding application.

PPP — Point-to-Point protocol handles error detection, supports multiple protocols, allows IP addresses to be negotiate at connection time, permits authentication, and has many other improvements over SLIP. While many internet service providers still support both SLIP and PPP, not only for dial-up lines, but also for leased router-router lines.

***PPP* (Point To Point Protocol)** — A protocol that provides a method for transmitting packets over serial point to point links. PPP is one of the most popular methods for dialup connections to the internet since it allows you to use other standard protocols over a standard telephone connection but it can also be used for LAN connections.

Pre-Data Warehouse The pre-data warehouse zone provides the data for data warehousing. Data warehouse designers determine which data contains business value for insertion.

Preemptive Scheduling With Preemptive scheduling a running process may be replaced by a higher priority process at any time. This is completed by activating the scheduler whenever an event that changes the state of the system is detected. Since such events include a number of actions in addition to the voluntary surrender of control by running process, preemption necessitates more frequent execution of the scheduler. Thus Preemptive scheduling is more responsive, but it puts higher overheads since each process rescheduling entails a complete process switch. Doing Preemptive scheduling requires having a clock interrupt occur at the end of the time interval to give control of the CPU back to the scheduler.

PREMO It stands for Presentation Environment for Multimedia Objects, and is an ISO standard being developed to provide a standardized development environment for multimedia applications. It concentrates mainly on presentation technique. One of the major goals of PREMO was to be able to integrate different media and their presentation techniques into the same framework.

Preprocessing Transformation of the input or target data before it is presented to the neural network.

PRE-SCAN A feature of many flatbed scanners that carry out a quick, low resolution scan to allow you to reposition the original or mark the area that is to be scanned at a higher resolution. to display the text or graphics on a screen as it will appear when it is printed out word

P

PREVIEW	processor ,such as Microsoft word have a standard view which allows you to type and edit rapidly . however if you want to see the effect of margins tables or columns you would switch to preview mode. Which shows exactly how page will look when printed?
Primary Index	Regardless of what form of index is used, every index must be updated whenever a record is either inserted into or deleted from the file. We describe algorithms for updating single-level indices Deletion: In order to delete a record, it is necessary to look up the record to be deleted. If the deleted record was the last record with its particular search key value, then we delete the search key value from the index. For dense indices, we delete a search key value similarly to deleting in a file. For sparse indices, we delete a key value by replacing its entry in index (if one exists) with the next search key value (in search-key order). If the next search key value already has an index entry, we delete the entry. Insertion: Perform a lookup using the search key value appearing in the record to be inserted. If the index is dense and the search key value does not appear in the index, insert it. If the index is sparse, no change needs to be made to the index unless a new block is created. In this case, the first search key value 9in search key order) appearing in the new block is inserted into the database.
PRIMARY KEY	to dente a candidate key that is chosen by data base designer as the principle means of identifying entities within an entity set.

Primary Key — It is a set of one or more attributes that can uniquely identify tuples within the relation. In some table, combination of more than one attribute provides a unique value for each row. In such tables, the group of these attribute is declared as primary key. In such cases, the primary key consists of more than on attribute, it is called composite primary key. The primary key is non-redundant.

Primary Memory Or Main Memory — It is a large memory which is fast but not as fast as internal processor memory. This memory is accessed directly by the processor. It is mainly based on integrated circuits.

Principal Component Analysis — Orthogonalize the components of network input vectors. This procedure can also reduce the dimension of the input vectors by eliminating redundant components.

PRINT — to produce characters on paper using ink or tonner.

PRINT OUT — the final printed page.

PRINT PREVIEW — a function of a software product that lets you see how a page will appear when printed.

PRINT SCREEN KEY — A key at the top right of key board that under DOS will send the characters on screen to printer. Under windows, its function has changed it now copies the screen image to the clip board if you want to print part of window screen press the print screen key. now start the paint program and choose the edit/ paste menu option a copy of the image that was displayed on the screen is copied into the paint file and can be printed or edited if you want to copy an image of active window rather than the whole screen press the alt and print screen key at the same time if you want to see what you have captured use the clip book viewer.

P

PRINTER a device that produce text or an image on paper using ink or toner under the control of a PC.

Priority Queue A queue does not operate on strictly FIFO (first In, First Out) basis. On the contrary, it stores the elements according to the priority associated with each stored element.

PROCEDURAL DML require a user to specify what data are needed and how to get those data.

Process Control Block: [Task Control Block/Job Control Block] PCB simply serves as the repository for any information that may vary from process to process. PCBs must be stored in monitor memory.

Process State A process program in execution. As the program executes the process changes state. Process execution is an alternating sequence of CPU and i/o bursts, beginning and ending with a CPU burst. Process states are new, active, waiting or halted.

PROCESSOR also called the central processing unit (CPU). It's an electronic device that contains millions of tiny components designed for basic arithmetic and control function. A CPU can add or subtract numbers, move numbers from one location to another, or control an external device. This is enough to do everything you see on your screen. Each of the actions of a CPU is controlled by an instruction. These are the machine control used to create s/w program. a CPUs speed (for example 2GHz) roughly defines the number of instructions that can be process each second -2 Billion in this case. The power of a CPU is also defined in its data-handling capabilities. A 32-bit CPU can add, subtract or manipulate numbers that are 32 bits wide. A 16-bit processor can only handle 16-bit numbers.

Products-Of-Sums (POS) A product-of-sums expression is a sum term (maxterm) or several sum terms (maxtrems) logically multiplied (AND-ed) together.)

Program Problem is a set of explicit and unambiguous instructions expressed in a programming language. This set of instructions is called a program.

Program 1) Complete set of instructions, y which direct a pc to carry out a particular task. A word processing package is thousands of separate instruction that respond to various actions. These instructions are written by a programmer. A program file normally has an extension of. EXE.

2) In MIDI, data that defined a sound in a synthesizer.

Program Control Register (PC) It holds the address of the next instruction to be executed. This register goes through a step-by-step counting sequence and causes the computer to read successive instructions, previously stored in memory.

Program Disk a disk containing software programs.

Program Icons An icon that represent a program file. To start the program, move the pointer over the icon and double-click.

Program Manager In windows, the name of the part of window the user sees. When you start windows you'll see a background and a main window with icon and smaller windows. This is the program manager and it allows you to format a disk, run an application or carry out similar basic housekeeping commands. In window 95,

Microsoft scrapped program manager. Instead the Screen is now taken up by the desktop.

Program Package 1) All of the computer files & instruction manual needed to run a program 2) descriptive of the qualities &capabilities that makes up a program. 3) A set of application as for various accounting function, that makes up a complete program.

Program Relocatability Feasibility of relocating a program and the manner in which relocation can be carried out characterizes a program into one of the following forms:

Non-relocatable programs

Relocatable programs

Self-relocation programs

Programme Restructuring This involves transforming a system from one representational form to another without a change in the semantics or functionality. Due to maintenance activities, the programs become complex and difficult to understand. To control this increase in complexity, the source code needs to be restructured. There are various types of restructuring techniques:

Control flow driven restructuring involves the imposition of a clear control structure within the source code can be either inter modular or intra-modular in nature.

Efficiency driven restructuring involves restructuring a function or algorithm to make it more efficient.

PROJECT METRICES model of s/w project metrics suggests that every project should measure

INPUTS measure of resources required to do work.

OUTPUT measures of deliverables or work products created during s/w engineering process.

RESULTS measures that indicate the effectiveness of deliverables.

s/w matrices materials are used for strategic process s/w project measures are tactical.

PROJECT PLANNING

It begins with the melding of problem &the process. each function to be engineered by the s/w team must pass through the set of frame work activities that have been designed for a s/w organization

1. *Customer* communication task required to establish effective communication between developer and customer.

2. *Planning* task required to define resources time lines, &other project related information.

3. *Risk* analysis task required to access both technical and management risks.

4. *Engineering* task required to build one or more representation of application.

5. *Construction* and release task required to construct text and install provide user support (ex: documentation and training).

6. *Customer* evaluation task required to obtain customer feedback based on evaluation of s/w representations created using engineering stage and implemented during installation stage.

PROLOG Programming

Prolog (stands for Programming in LOGIC). It uses the syntax of predicate logic to perform symbolic, logical computations. Programming in PROLOG is completed by creating a database of facts and rules about objects, their properties & their relationships to other objects. Queries can be posed about the objects and valid conclusions will be determined and returned by the program.

Prompt A message that appears on the monitor while a network system is waiting for you to enter a command or option.

Properties In window 95, the attributes of a file or object. To view or edit all the properties of a file, select the file with a single click to highlight the name and click once on the right –hand mouse button. This display a small menu of option. Select the properties of a file, select the properties menu option and you will see the various properties for the object. if the object is a file, you can view or edit the attributes to make the file read-only or hidden. You can location of an object.

Protection If paging or segmentation is provided, different sections of a user program can be declared execute only, read only, or read-write. This restriction is necessary with stored code or data, and is generally useful in any case to provide simple runtime checks for common programming errors.

Protocol Simply, the "language' spoken between computer to help them exchange information .More technically, it's a normal description of message formats and the rules that computer must follow to exchange those messages. Protocols can describe low-level details of machine-to-machine interface (like the order in which bits and bytes are sent across a wire) or high-level-exchanges between allocation programs (the way in which two programs transfer a file across the internet).

PrtSc Stands for print screen on an IBM pc keyboard. Key that sends the content of the current of the current screen to the printer or copies a window screen a windows screen to the clipboard.

Public Key Encryption In many encryption schemes, the key must be kept secret to avoid compromising security. One particularly interesting encryption technique assigns each user a pair of keys. One of the user's keys, called the private key, is kept secret, while the other, called the public key, is published along with the name of the user, so everyone knows the value of the key. The encryption function has the mathematical property that a message encrypted with the public key cannot be easily decrypted except with the private key and a message encrypted with the private key cannot be decrypted except with the public key.

Pull-Down Menu A set of options display below an entry on a menu bar. If you click on the start button in windows 95 you'll see an example of a pull-down menu.

Purge To empty the contents of the recycle bin in windows an entry on a menu bar. If you click on the bin to highlight it, then click on the right-hand mouse button and choose the empty option.

Q

QBE (Query-By-Example)	QBE is a graphical query language based on domain calculus. Queries are formulated in QBE by generating on a skeleton table an example of what the user wishes to retrieve.
QFD (Quality Function Deployment)	It is quality management technique that translates the needs of the customer into technical requirements for software.
Quad-Speed Drive	CD-ROM drive that spins the disc at four times the speed of a single-speed drive providing higher data throughput of 600Kbps and shorter seek time, which means you go to where more quickly. Quad –speed drive are now standard on most new PCs in high-performance PCs they have been superseded by six-speed drives.
Qualities Of Information	Qualities of the information to be provided to managers are Accurate: Ensure correct input and processing rules Complete: include all data Trustworthy: Do not hide unpleasant information Timely: Give at right time Up to date: Include all data up to present time Relevant: Understand user needs Brief: Summarize relevant information Significant understandable: use attractive format and graphical charts.
Quantize	1) to convert an analogue signal into a numerical representation. 2) To process a MIDI file and align all the notes to a regular beat, removing any timing errors.

quasi-Newton Algorithm Class of optimization algorithm based on Newton's method. An approximate Hessian matrix is computed at each iteration of the algorithm based on the gradients.

Query A statement requesting the retrieval of information.

Query Window 1) window that appears when an error has occurred, asking the user what action you like to take. 2) Window that is displayed with field you can fill in to search a database.

Queue A queue may be defined as an ordered group of elements in which new elements are added at one end called the rear and elements are removed at the other end called the front.

Quick-Fix Model This is basically an ad-hoc approach to maintain software. This model waits for the problem to occur and then tries to fix it as quickly as possible. In this model, fixes would be done without detailed analysis of the long term effects, for example, ripple effects through the software or effects on the code structure. There would be little, if any documentation. Where are the advantages of such a model and why it is still used? In an appropriate environment it can work perfectly well.

Quicksort Or Partition Exchange Sort **Quicksort** or **partition-exchange sort**, is a sorting algorithm developed by Tony Hoare that, on average, makes $O(n \log n)$ comparisons to sort n items. In the worst case, it makes $O(n^2)$ comparisons, though this behavior is rare. Quicksort is often faster in practice than other $O(n \log n)$ algorithms. Additionally, quicksort's sequential and localized memory references work well with a cache. Quicksort is a comparison sort and, in efficient implementations, is not a stable sort.

Q

Quicksort can be implemented with an in-place partitioning algorithm, so the entire sort can be done with only O(log *n*) additional space used by the stack during the recursion.

QWERTY Keyboard English –language keyboard layout for a typewriter or computer, in which the top line of letter are QWERTY. The French use a different layout with the top line reading AZERTY.

R

RAD Model Rapid application development is a linear sequential s/w development process model that emphasizes an extremely short development cycle. It is a "high-speed" adaptation of the linear sequential model in which rapid development is achieved by using a component –based construction approach. RAD Approach encompasses 1. Business modeling 2.data modeling. 3. Process modeling. 4. Application generation 5.testing &turnover.

Radial Basis Networks Neural network that can be designed directly by fitting special response

elements where they will do the most good.

Radix Sort **Radix sort** is a non-comparative integer sorting algorithm that sorts data with integer keys by grouping keys by the individual digits which share the same significant position and value. A positional notation is required, but because integers can represent strings of characters (e.g., names or dates) and specially formatted floating point numbers, radix sort is not limited to integers.

Ragged text that is not starting or that an uneven edge.

RAM stands for random access memory .This memory allows access to any location in any order ,without having to access the rest first. the memory chips in your PC are RAM ,since any location can be accessed by specifying its address . a magnetic tape is not random access since you must read through all location before you reach the one you want.

R

RAM Cache	Memory used to store data that is often called into use. on a video card, for example, the RAM cache may hold the window that are hidden from view in order to provide rapid screen refresh when the window is brought into view.
Rambaughs Method	The OMT for analysis, system design & object-level design Rambaugh's OOA process follow 1 develop a statement of scope for the problem. 2 build an object model. 3 develop a dynamic model. 4 construct a functional model for the system.
RAMDAC(Random Access Memory Digital To Analog Converter)	A chip that converts digital data from the computer to analog data used by certain other devices, such as a monitor screen.
Real Time	Processing time, which is of the same order of magnitude as the problem to be solved? This means the PC can solve a problem in a certain time and its result can influence the source of the data. Air-traffic control computers have to analyze the position of aircraft within a second so that do not collide. If the computer was not working in real time, it would spend ten minutes calculating the action.
Real- Time Animation	Pc animation in which objects appear to move just as they would in real life.
Re-Boot	The equivalent of switching your PC off then on. You can reboot using the ctrl-alt-del key combination or by choosing the start/ shutdown/reboot in windows 95.
Record	The units of data used for buffering. It may be a physical record (such as a line image for a printer or a character from a keyboard or a block from a tape or disk) or it may be a logical record (such as an input line, an English word or an array)

Record A set of data relating to a specific thing (e.g. person, car, etc.). The data are identified by field names.

Record-Base Logical Models Are so named because the database is structure in fixed-format record of several type. Each record type defines a fixed number of fields, or attributes, & each field is usually of a fixed length.

Recycle Bin An icon that's displayed on windows 95 desktop that look like a wastepaper bin. If you want to delete a file or folder, drag it on to the recycle bin or press the delete key. The recycle bin stores the file or folder for a certain number of days or until you purge it.

Refresh The process of regularly updating the images on a screen by scanning each pixel with a pitcher beam to make sure the image is still visible. The image on the screen is visible because tiny dots of phosphor shine. The glow from the phosphor only a few tenths of a seconds is repeated 60 to 70 times per second.

Register Registers are temporary storage places and holds data, addresses etc., for doing operations on them for data transfer. The important registers are

Memory Address Register (MAR)

Memory Buffer Register (MBR)

Program Control Register (PC)

Accumulator Register (A)

Instructions Register

Input / Output Register

Registry A database that forms the basis of window 95 and contains information about every program stores on the disk and the users, network and preferences. You'll never see the registry, but it's worth knowing it's there in case you see an error messages such as object not found in registry. This means some program has not been correctly installed.

Regression Testing Each time a new module is added to integration testing, the software changes. New data flow paths are established, new I/O may occur, and new control logic is invoked. These changes can cause problems with functions that earlier worked without flow. In the context of an integration test strategy, regression testing is the re-execution of some subset of tests that have already been conducted to see that changes have not caused unintended side effects.

Regular Expression In theoretical computer science and formal language theory, a regular expression is a sequence of characters that forms a search pattern, mainly for use in pattern matching with strings, or string matching, i.e. "find and replace"-like operations.

Regular Expression Processor A regular expression processor processes a regular expression statement expressed in terms of a grammar in a given formal language, and with that examines the target text string, parsing it to identify substrings that are members of its language, the regular expressions.

Regular Languages A languages 'L' is called regular if and only if there exists some deterministic finite accepter M such that L = L (M).

Regularization Modification of the performance function, which is normally chosen to be the sum of squares of the network errors on the training set, by adding some fraction of the squares of the network weights.

Relational Data Model In relational model, the data is organized into tables. These tables are called relations. A row in a table represents a relationship among a set of values. Since a table is a collection of such relationship.

Reliability Is evaluated by measuring the frequency &severity of failure, the accuracies of output results, the mean time between failures (MTBF), the ability to recover from failure, & the predictability of the program.

Relocatable Program A relocatble program from is one which consists of a program and relevant information for its relocation. Using this information, it is possible to relocate the program to execute from a storage area other than the one designated for it at the time of its coding or translation. The relocation information would identify address sensitive portions of code indicate how they can be relocated.

Relocation One solution to the external fragmentation problem is compaction. Compaction involves shifting a programming memory without the program noticing the change. This consideration requires that logical address be relocated dynamically, at load time, we cannot compact storage.

Renaming To change the name of a file or a folder. In windows 95, click once on the files or folder that you want to rename and keep the pointer over the icon. After a couple of second the description will be surrounded by box and you can now edit the name. In DOS use the REN command, and in windows 3.1x use the file manager utility.

Repeater Repeater is an hardware device which is operated on the physical layer. Repeater installed on a link receives the signal before it becomes too weak or corrupted, regenerates the original bits patterns and put the refreshed copy back on the link. The repeater does not change the functionality of the network.

Replay To play back or a signal from a recording.

REQUIRMENT Analysis It is a software engineering task that bridges the gap between system level software allocation &s\w design. Software requirements analysis may be divided into 5 areas of effort. 1.Problems recognition. 2. Evaluation &synthesis. 3. Modeling. 4. Specification. 5. Re view.

Resilient Back Propagation Training algorithm that eliminates the harmful effect of having a small slope at the extreme ends of the sigmoid squashing transfer functions.

Resolution 1) number of pixels that a screen or printer can display per unit area. 2)difference between two levels that can be differentiated in a digitized signal.3) degree of accuracy with which something can be measured or timed.

Resource an on-line information set or an on-line interactive option. An on-line library catalog or the local school lunch menus are example of information sets. On-line menus or graphical user interfaces, internet, e –mail, on –line conferences, telnet, FTP, and gopher are example of interactive options.

Response A message placed in a conference as a follow-up to a topic or to another response; or, a reply to an e-mail message.

RET (Resolution Enhancement Technology) A technique developed by Hewlett-Packard to smooth the rough edge of a printed image & improve its resolution.

RGB In color TV there three color guns producing red, green and blue beams acting on group of three phosphor dots in each pixel.

1) high-definition monitor system that uses three separate input signals controlling red, green and blue color picture beam.

2) The three-color pitcher beam used in color TV.

Rich Text Format (RFT) — a way of storing a document that includes all the commands that describe the page, front and formatting. The RFT format allows formatted pages to be exchanged between different words processors.

Ring Structure File Organization — A ring is simply a linear list that closes upon itself. In terms of the definition of a K-list, the beginning and end of the list are the same record. This data-structure is particularly useful to show classification of data.

RMMM Plan — Risk mitigation monitoring &management plan the RMMM Plan document all work performed as part of risk analysis &is used by the project manager as part of the overall project plan

ROM. Read-Only Memory — Information is stores once, usually by the manufacture that cannot be changed. Most compact disc are ROM.

Root Directory — the topmost directory from which all other directories branch. In the DOS and OS/2 and Unix operating system, this is represented as a single backslash character. For example, if you want to move to root directory, you would issue the CD\command in DOS. Confusingly, the root directory actually represents the top of the tree structure, mixing part of the same metaphor. As you move from the root directory to the sub-directories, you are moving into branches.

Round-Robin Scheduling It is more appropriate for a time-shared system. It allocates the CPU to the first process in the ready queue for 'q' time units, where 'q' is the time quantum. After 'q' time units, the CPU are preempted and the process is put at the tail of the ready queue. The Major problem is selections of the time quantum.

Router A devices for linking an ISDM line to a LAN so that the digital signals can be sent to the appropriate computer on the LAN.

Router It is an internetworking device. It operates at network layer. Router routes packet between potentially different networks. It is very sophiscated device because it contains the software and can take a decision to choose best path for data transmission. It is basically used for inter-networking. It transfer, accepts and relays packet only across networks using similar protocol.

Routing The real function of the network layer is routing packets from the source machine to the destination machine.

Routing Algorithm It is the part of the network layer software responsible for deciding which output line an incoming packet should be transmitted on. If the subnet uses datagram internally, this decision must be made a new for every arriving data packet. Routing algorithms are of two types:

Non-adaptive: these algorithms do not base their routing decisions on measurement or estimates of the current traffic and topology.

Adaptive: These algorithms in contrast follow the above concept.

RTN (Recursive Transition Networks) It is a transition network which permits are labels to refer to other network (including the networks own name) & they turn may refer back to referring network rather than just permitting word categories used previously.

Run Command In windows this command lets you type in the name of a program that you want to run or a DOS commands you want to execute. To enter a command, select the.

S

SADT Structure analysis &design technique is a technique that has been widely used as notation for system definition, process representations, software requirements analysis & system design.

Safe Mode A special operation mode of window 95 that is selected if window detects a problems when starting .safe mode does not let you do anything except try to work out and fix the problems. When you first install window 95 you should create a safe mode floppy disk that contains the configuration details for your PC. If nothing else work, window will ask you to insert this disk and will copy the initial setting over.

SAFETY Algorithm The algorithm for finding out whether a system is in a safe state or not [to know the system is in deadlock state or not]

Sample A measurement of signals at a point in time, normally used to describe the action of a soundcard that is converting a sound or noise into a form that can be stored on disk.

SAP Service Access Points

Satellite Processing The small computer was a satellite of the main computer satellite processing was one of the first cases of multiple computer systems working together to improve performance

Save To store a document on a disk. Window Application have a ctrl-shortcut for this function or you can choose the file/save menu option.

Save As This lets you save a named document to disk under a different name or in a different format. If you have written a message in Microsoft word and want to save it in plain text format so that it can be sent as email, you would select the file/save as menu option.

Scalable Front A front that can be displayed or printed at any size without changing shape each letter is described as a set of curve which can be altered to print at any size without looking jagged

Scaled Conjugate Gradient Algorithm Avoids the time-consuming line search of the standard conjugate gradient algorithm.

Scan 1) To convert a printer image or photo into a digital form. 2) to move a picture beam across a screen, one line at a time, to refresh the image on the screen.3) to convert an optical image into a digital form by examining each pixel on a line of a frame, then moving down one line.

Scandisk A utility supplied with MS-DOS (which is also part of window 95) that will check your hard disk for problems.

Scanner A device which uses photo-electric cells to convert a drawing, photograph or document into data which can be manipulated by a pc. A flat-bed scanner has a flat sheet of glass on which the image is place. The scan head moves below the glass. A hand-held scanner is held in your hand and contains a row of photo electric cell which, moved over an image, convert it into data.

Scenario-Based Test Design Scenario-based testing concentrates on what the user does not what the product does. It means capturing the task that the user has to perform, then applying them &their variants as test. Scenario describes two things a test &specific user needs.

Scheduler A scheduler is an operating system module that selects the next job to be admitted into the system and then the next process to run.

S

A set of policies and mechanisms built into the operating system that govern the order in which the work to be done by the computer system is completed, this is allied scheduling.

Scheduling Algorithm Scheduling algorithm can be divided into two categories with respect to how they deal with clock interrupts. These two categories are:

1. Preemptive
2. Non-Preemptive

SCM software configuration management is an umbrella activity that is applied throughout the software process. Because change can occur at any time, SCM activity are developed to. 1) Identify change. 2)control change. 3) Ensure that change is being properly implement .4) report change to other who may have an interest

Scratchpad Memory A section of high-speed memory chips that are used to buffer data being transferred between a fast processor and a slow i/o devices such as a disk drive

Screen 1) A display device capable of showing an image. 2) Grid of dots or lines placed between a camera and artwork, which has the effect of dividing the picture up into small dots, creating an image, which can be used for printing.

Screen Capture to store an image displayed on screen in a file. This is useful when creating manuals about a software product. In windows you can capture the current screen to the clipboard by pressing the print screen key.

Screen Saver Software which, after a period of inactivity, replaces the existing image on screen and display moving object to protect against screen burn

Scroll Bar a bar display along the side of windows with a maker, which indicates how far you have scrolled

Scsi(Small Computer System Interface) A computer that transfer data at high speed & supports multiple peripherals through a signal PC expansion slot.

SDU Service Data Unit

Search a function that allows you to look through a data base or document for a word or phrases

Search Engines It is the programs, which accept a string as input and will output the entire URL's whose pages contain related information to the string. A few search engines are GOOGLE, DOGPILE, YAHOO, EXCITE, INFOSEEK, LOOKSMART, LYCOS, WEBCRAWLER etc.,

Second 66 million in this case. The power of a CPU is also defined in its data- handling capabilities. A 32-bit CPU can add, subtract or manipulate number that is 32 bits wide. A 16-bit process can only handle 16-bit number.

Second Normal Form A relation scheme is said to be in 2NF if it is in the 1NF and if all non-key attributes are fully functionally dependent on the primary key.

Secondary Indices This approach allows all the pointers for one secondary search key value to be stored together. Such an approach is useful in certain types of queries for which keys, we can obtain all the pointers for one primary search key value using a sequential scan. A sequential scan in primary key order is efficient because records are stored physically in an order that approximates primary key order. However, we cannot store a file physically ordered both by the primary key and by a secondary key.

Because secondary key order and physical key order differ, if we attempt to scan the file sequentially in secondary key order, the reading of each record is likely to require the reading of a new block form disk.

Secondary Key It is an attribute or combination of attributors that may not be a candidate key but classify the entity set on particular characteristics.

Secondary Memory Auxiliary memory is much larger in size than main memory but is slower than main memory. It normally stores system programs other instructions, programs and data files. Secondary memory can also be used as an overflow memory in case the main memory capacity has been exceeded. Secondary memories cannot be accessed directly by a processor. First the information of these memories is transferred to the main memory and then the information can be accessed as the information of main memory.

Sector the smallest area on magnetic disk, which can be addressed by PC. The disk is divided into concentric tracks, is divided into sectors which can store 512 bytes of data

Security The availability of mechanisms that control or protect programs & data.

Security Testing It's an attempt to verify that protection mechanisms built into a system will in fact protect it from improper penetration

Seek Time The average times it takes to position a hard disk read/write head over data being sought.

Select 1) to position a pointer over an object, such as a button or menu option and click on the mouse-button. 2) To find and retrieve specific information from a database.

Selection Sort In computer science, **selection sort** is a sorting algorithm, specifically an in-place comparison sort. It has $O(n^2)$ time complexity, making it inefficient on large lists, and generally performs worse than the similar insertion sort. Selection sort is noted for its simplicity, and it has performance advantages over more complicated algorithms in certain situations, particularly where auxiliary memory is limited.

The algorithm divides the input list into two parts: the sub list of items already sorted, which is built up from left to right at the front (left) of the list, and the sub list of items remaining to be sorted that occupy the rest of the list. Initially, the sorted sub list is empty and the unsorted sub list is the entire input list. The algorithm proceeds by finding the smallest (or largest, depending on sorting order) element in the unsorted sub list, exchanging it with the leftmost unsorted element (putting it in sorted order), and moving the sub list boundaries one element to the right.

Self-Documentation The degree to which the source code provider meaningful documentation

Self-Relocating Program A self-relocating program is one which can itself perform the relocation of its address sensitive portions. Thus, it not only contains information regarding its address sensitivity but also the code to make use of this information to relocate the address sensitive part of its code. Such a program does not need an external agency like the linkage editor to relocate it. It can be simply loaded into its load area and given control for execution. Prior to execution of its main code, the simply loaded into its load area and given control for execution. Prior to execution of its main code, the relocating logic would be executed to adopt the program to its execution time storage addresses.

SEMAPHOES Used to solve various synchronization problems and they can be implemented efficiently it's a solutions for all require busy-waiting.

Sequential File Organization Records are stored in sequential order based on the value of the search key each record.

Sequential Files A sequential file is the most primitive of all file structures. It has no directory and no linking pointers. The records are generally organized in lexicographic order on the value of some key. In other words, a particular attribute is chosen whose value will determine the order of the records. Sometimes when the attribute value is constant for a large number of records a second key is chosen to give an order when the first key fails to discriminate.

Sequential Input Vectors Set of vectors that are to be presented to a network one after the other. The network weights and biases are adjusted on the presentation of each input vector.

Sequential Searching See the **Linear search.**

Server A dedicated computer which provides a function to a network such as storing images, or printing data.

Service(Or Service Provider) An organization that provides access to part of the internet. You have to arrange for an account with a service to connect your computer to the internet.

Session The time period between when you "log in" to and "log off" from a network system.

Sets A set is a collection of elements without any structure other than membership.

SGML Standard Generalized Markup Language is in ISO standard markup language for text. It is used to write Document Type Definitions (DTDs) which are descriptions of classes of structured information.

Shared Folder If your pc is connected to a network, you can declare that a folder can be used by other user on the network to share a folder, click once on the folder icon and the click on the right-hand mouse button. Select the properties option from the pop-up menu and choose sharing. Once you have set a folder as shareable, the icon for the folder changes so that it now appears with a cable running below the folder to remind you that other users have access to it.

Share-Level Access A way of setting up network security to protect your local resources this means that each resource, such as a printer ,file or folder that you want to share with other users on the network can be protected by a password. The alternative to share-level access is called user-level access. Windows for workgroups and windows 95 both let you set up share-level access for small network of two or more PCs.

Shareware Software which is available free for you to sample. But if you keep it you are expected to pay a fee to the writer. Often confused with public-domain software, which is completely free.

Sharing It generally requires that either paging or segmentation be used to provide small packets of information (pages or segments) which can be sharing is a means of running many users with a limited amount of memory but shared programs and data must be carefully designed.

S

SHEAR A transformation that distorts the shape of an object such that the transformed shape appears as if the object were composed of internal layers that had been caused to slide over each other is caller a shear. Two common shearing transformations are those that shift coordinate x values and those that shift y values.

Shell Software which operates between the user and the operating system, often to try to make the operating system more friendly or easier to use. For example, MS-DOS'S COMMAND. COM is a basic shell that interpret commands type in at the prompt. Window 95 is sophisticated shell with a graphical user interface front-end that's operated by a mouse.

Short Remaining Time Next (SRTN) Scheduling In this scheduling, a job or a process, is selected on the basis of the shortest remaining execution time. It may be implemented either in preemptive or non-preemptive version. The SRTN is one of the optical scheduling disciplines that minimize the average waiting time of the system.

Shortcut An icon placed on the desktop in windows 95 that links to a file, folder or program stored on the disk. The shortcut has the same icon as the original files except for tiny arrows in the bottom left-hand corner. The shortcut is not a duplicate of the original, rather it is a pointer to the original.

Shortest-Job-First Scheduling It is provably optimal, providing the shortest average waiting time. It is difficult to implement because it is difficult to predict the length of the next CUPs first. SJF is a special case of the general priority scheduling algorithm, which simply allocates the CUPs to the highest priority process. Both priority and scheduling may suffer from starvation. Aging is a technique to prevent starvation.

Shut Down When you want to switch off your pc, you should first windows 95. This ensures that all the files are closed and the windows sorts itself out internally before being

SIG Acronym for Special Interest Group. SIGs sponsor a variety of List serves, IRC channels, and Internet sites, Also a nickname for a Signature.

Sigma Parameter Determines the change in weight for the calculation of the approximate Hessian matrix in the scaled conjugate gradient algorithm.

Signature An ASCII text file that can be automatically attached to the bottom of a piece of email or newsgroup posting that identifies the sender. Many signatures (or sigs) use symbols and characters to create images or words to make the sig more interesting.

SIMD Single Instruction and Multiple Data Streams. SIMD machines are especially designed to perform vector computations over matrices or arrays of data.

Simple Network Management Protocol (SNMP) It is an "Internet-Standard protocol for managing devices on IP networks". Devices that typically support SNMP include routers, switches, servers, workstations, printers, modem racks and more. It is used mostly in network management systems to monitor network-attached devices for conditions that warrant administrative attention. SNMP is a component of the Internet Protocol Suite as defined by the Internet Engineering Task Force (IETF). It consists of a set of standards for network management, including an application layer protocol, a database schema, and a set of data objects. SNMP exposes management data in the form of variables on the managed systems, which describe the system configuration. These variables can then be queried (and sometimes set) by managing applications.

Simplicity The degree to which a program can be understood without difficulty

Simulation Takes the network input p, and the network object net, and returns the network outputs a.

Sleep If you have installed power management on your PC you will find that it shuts down some sections of the computer, such as the hard disk and monitor, after a period of inactivity. These devices are sleeping and will be powered up again as soon as you touch the mouse or hit a key.

Smart Card These cards contain microprocessors having memories. It has an encrypted key which is compared to the other secret key stored in the customer's computer. Immediately on making purchase out of smart card the equivalent money value is taken out from the smart card.

Smiley The use of punctuation marks and other symbols or characters to portray moods when typing, especially in email messages and IRC. Here's an example of a simple smiley: :). If you don't see it, till your head to the left and look at it. The colon makes the eyes and the parenthesis makes the smiley mouth. The smile means happiness (like if someone says some funny) or it often denotes sarcasm. Other combinations of characters can express many other emotions. You may also hear them referred to as emotions.

SMTP (Simple Mail Transfer Protocol) A protocol used to transfer email. SMTP transfers mail from server to server, and the end user must use POP (see also post office protocol)to transfers the messages to their machine.

SNMP (Simple Network Management Protocol) Developed to manage nodes on an IP network, SNMP is an internet standard protocol. It can be used to manage wiring hubs, video toasters, CD ROM jukeboxes, and many other devises.

SNMP MODEL Simple network management protocol model of a managed network consists of 4 components

Managed Nodes

Management Stations

Management Information

A Management Protocol

Snow Interference or a fault with a screen that's apparent us flickering white flecks.

Soft Copy An electronic version of a file, usually in computer memory and/or an disk; as opposed to hard copy, the paper print out.

Software Computer programs that performs various tasks. Word processing programs (like WordPerfect or Microsoft Word), spreadsheet programs (like lotus or excel), or data base programs (like dbase III+, FoxBASE, or Oracle) are all software.

Software System Independence The degree to which the program is independent of nonstandard programming language feature, operating system characteristic &other environmental constants.

S

Software Agents	It represents a new technology with the potential to become one of the most important tools of information technology in the twenty first century. The software agents can alleviate the most critical limitation of the internet-information overflow and can facilitate electronic commerce.
Software Applications	System software, Real-time software , Business software, Engineering and scientific software, Embedded software, Personal Computer software, Artificial Intelligence software
Software Design	It's a process of applying various techniques and principles for purpose of defining a device, a process, a system insufficient detail to permit its physical realization. It is a multi-step process that focuses on 4 distinct attributes of a program. They are Data Structure or Data design: Transforms information domain model created during analysis into data structures that will be required to implement software. Software Architecture: Defines relationship among major structural elements of program Interface representation: Describes how software communicates with itself, with other systems and with humans who use it. Procedural design: Transforms structural components into procedural description of software components.
Software Equations (SE)	It is multivariable model that assumes a specific distribution of effort over the life of a Software development project. E = [Loc*B^0.333/P]^3 * [1/t^4]

Where E= effort in person-months or person-years, t= project duration in months or years B= "special skills factor" that increases slowly as "the need for integration, testing, quality assurance, documentation, and management skills grow", P="productivity parameter".

Software License An agreement between a user and a software house, giving details of the right of the user to use or copy software.

Software Measurement (SM) Measurement in the physical world can be categorized in two ways: Direct measures (example, the length of a bolt) and indirect measures (example, the "quality" of bolts produced, measured by counting rejects).

Software Metrics Defined as "The continuous application of measurement based techniques to the software development process and its products to supply meaningful and timely management information together with the use of those techniques to improve that process and its products".

Software Quality Assurance It is an umbrella activity that is applied throughout the software process. It includes:

A quality management approach

Effective software engineering technology (methods and tools)

Formal technical reviews that are applied throughout the software process

A multi-tiered testing strategy

Control of software documentation and the changes made to it.

A procedure to ensure compliance with software development standards (when applicable).

Measurement and reporting mechanisms.

S

Software Re-Engineering

Software re-engineering encompasses a series of activities that include:

Inventory analysis

Document restructuring

Reverse engineering

Code restructuring

Data restructuring

Forward engineering

Software Team

The "first" team structure depends on the management style of an organization, the number of peoples who will populate the team and their skill levels and the overall problems difficulty. Manti [MAN81] suggest three generic team organizations:

Democratic Decentralized (DD): These software engineering team has no permanent leader rather, "task co-coordinator are appointed for short duration and then replaced by others who may co-ordinate difference task". Decisions on problem and approach are made by group consensus. Communication among team members is horizontal.

Controlled Decentralized (CD): This software engineering team has a defined leader who co-ordinates specific tasks and secondary leaders that have responsibility for subtask problem solving remains a group activity, but implementation of solutions is partitioned among subgroups by the team leader. Communication among subgroups and individuals in horizontal. Vertical communication along the control hierarchy also accurse.

Controlled centralized (CC): Top level problem solving and internal team co-ordination are managed by team leader. Communication between the leader and team members in vertical.

Software Testing It is a critical element of a software quality assurance and represents the ultimate review of specification, design and coding.

Software Testing Principles A software engineer must understand basic principles that guide software testing before designing test cases. The various testing principles given by Davis are

All tests should be traceable to customer requirements

Tests should be planned long before testing begins.

The Pareto principle applies to software testing.

Testing should begin "in the small" and progress towards testing "in the large".

Exhaustive testing is not possible.

To be most effective, testing should be conducted by third party.

Solid Color A color that can be displayed on a screen or printer on a color printer without dithering.

Sound File A file stored on disk that contains sound data. This can either be a digitized analogue sound signal or notes for a MIDI instrument.

Sound Recorder A utility included with Windows that allows you to play bake digitized sound file (the .WAV standard) or record sound on to disk and carry out very basic editing once you have recorded the sound.

Soundcard An add-on device that plugs in to an expansion slot inside your PC and generates analogue sound signals. The soundcard generates sound from digital data, using either a digital or analogue converter or a FM synthesis chip. Also provide function to recorded sound in digital form (using an analogue to digital converter) and control MID instruments. Unlike Apple Macs, PCs do not come with built in sound generation hardware, so to produce you need to fit a soundcard. There are three major standards for PC soundcards: Adlib, SoundBlaster and Windows-compatible. The MPC Level 1 specification states that a soundcard should be able to record sound in eight bits and sample at 11.025 KHz. Some soundcards provide built-in compression for wave file, but there are various methods used. The MPC recommends ADCMP. In addition many PC soundcards include electronics to generate sound from MID data on board. There are two kinds of MID sound generation. FM synthesis simulates musical notes by modulating the frequency of base carrier waves, whereas wave form synthesis uses digitized samples of the nodes the produce a more realistic sound.

Space Overhead The additional space occupied by an index structure. Provided that the amount of additional space is moderate, it is usually worthwhile to sacrifice the space to achieve improved performance.

Spanning Tree A tree is a connected undirected graph with no cycles. It is a spanning tree of a graph *G* if it spans *G* (that is, it includes every vertex of *G*) and is a sub graph of *G* (every edge in the tree belongs to *G*). A spanning tree of a connected graph *G* can also be defined as a maximal set of edges of G that contains no cycle, or as a minimal set of edges that connect all vertices.

Sparse Index Index records are created for only some of the records. To locate a record, we find the index record with the largest search key value that is less than or equal to the search-key value for which we are looking. We start at the record pointed to by that index record and follow the pointers in the file until we find the desired record.

Sparse Matrices In the subfield of numerical analysis, a **sparse matrix** is a matrix populated primarily with zeros as elements of the table. By contrast, if a larger number of elements differ from zero, then it is common to refer to the matrix as a **dense matrix**. The fraction of zero elements (non-zero elements) in a matrix is called the **sparsity** (**density**).

When storing and manipulating sparse matrices on a computer, it is beneficial and often necessary to use specialized algorithms and data structures that take advantage of the sparse structure of the matrix. Operations using standard dense-matrix structures and algorithms are relatively slow and consume large amounts of memory when applied to large sparse matrices. Sparse data is by nature easily compressed, and this compression almost always results in significantly less computer data storage usage. Indeed, some very large sparse matrices are infeasible to manipulate using standard dense algorithms.

Speaker Adaptive System A speaker adaptive system is developed to adapt its operation to the characteristics of new speakers. Its difficulty lies somewhere between speaker independent and speaker dependent systems.

S

Speaker Dependent System — A speaker dependent system is developed to operate for a single speaker. These systems are usually easier to develop, cheaper to buy and more accurate, then but not as flexible as speaker adaptive or speaker independent systems.

Speaker Identification — Given a known set of speakers, the identities of the input voice can be told. The task of the system is to find out which of the training speakers made the test utterance. So, the output of the system is the name of the training speaker, or possibly a rejection if the utterance has been made by a unknown person. On the other hand, identification is the task of determining an unknown speaker's identity; we can say it is a 1: N match where the voice compared against N templates.

Speaker Independent System — A speaker independent system is developed to operate for *any* speaker of a particular type (e.g. American English). These systems are the most difficult to develop, most expensive and accuracy is lower than speaker dependent systems. However, they are more flexible.

Speaker Verification — The verification task, or 1:1 matching, consists of making a decision whether a given voice sample is produced by a claimed speaker. An identity claim (e.g., a PIN code) is given to the system, and the unknown speaker's voice sample is compared against the claimed speaker's voice template. If the similarity degree between the voice sample and the template exceeds a predefined decision threshold, the speaker is accepted, and otherwise rejected. (the expected result is a yes or no decision).

Special Cases — See the Error guessing

Speech Application An application in which users interact with the program by speaking. Speech application is a broad term, but usually it runs separately from the speech platform and the speech engine.

Speech Engine The software program that recognizes speech. A speech engine takes a spoken utterance, compares it to the vocabulary, and matches the utterance to vocabulary words.

Speech Platform A piece of software that runs the speech application. It follows the logic of the application, collects spoken audio, passes the audio to the speech engine, and passes the recognition results back to the application.

Speech Recognition The process by which a computer speech engine recognizes human speech.

Speech recognition (SR) is technology that can translate spoken words into text. Some SR systems use "training" where an individual speaker reads sections of text into the SR system. These systems analyze the person's specific voice and use it to fine tune the recognition of that person's speech, resulting in more accurate transcription. Systems that do not use training are called "Speaker Independent" systems. Systems that use training are called "Speaker Dependent" systems.

Speech Recognition Analyzing spoken words so that a PC can recognize them.

Speech Recognition Grammar Specification (SRGS) A W3C standard for writing grammars. SRGS grammars can be written in two main formats: ABNF and grXML, both of which are equivalent to one another. Grammars may be easily translated between the two formats.

S

Spell Check

A function of word processors and DTP programs that checks the spelling of words by comparing them with words in a dictionary file. The spell check function can sometimes include a thesaurus that will display similar words to the miss pelt word or a sound-like function that displays words that sound the same but have different spellings.

Spiral Model

It couples the interactive nature of prototyping with the controlled and systematic aspects of the linear sequential model. It is divided into number of framework activities, also called task regions. It contains and task region

Customer Communication: tasks required to establish effective communication between developer and customer.

Planning: Tasks required defining resources, timelines and other project related information.

Risk analysis: Tasks required to assess both technical and management risks.

Engineering: Tasks required building one or more representations of the applications.

Construction and Released: Tasks required to construct, test, install and provide user support (example, documentation and training)

Customer evolution: Task required to obtained customer feedback based on evolution of the Software representation created during the engineering stage and implemented during the installation stage.

Spooler

A hardware or Software device that can be used to store computer output so that it can be piped to the printer in sequential order with little or no disturbance to for ground processing, or to be printed at a last time.

Spooling Abbreviation Simultaneous Peripheral Operation On-Line. Spooling essentially uses the disk as a very large buffer, for reading as for ahead as possible on input devices and for storing output files until the output devices are able to accept them.

Spread Constant Distance an input vector must be from a neuron's weight vector to produce an output of 0.5.

SQL (Structured Query Language) A type of computer standard for retrieving database records from a remote database.

SSI (Small Scale Integration) The process of designing a few circuits on a single chip. The term refers to the technology used to fabricate discrete logic gates on a chip.

Stack An area of memory in RAM reserved for the temporary storage of data, 'stacked' in the order it was last called. This stacking technique, designed to improve computer performance, is based on the theory that the items called most recently are among those most likely to be called again soon.

Star Learning Rule Learning rule that trains a neuron's weight vector to take on the values of the current input vector. Changes in the weights are proportional to the neuron's output.

Start Button A button that is normally found in the bottom left-hand corner of a Windows desktop screens. The start button provides a convenient route to the programs and files stored on your computer. The start button has categories for programs, accessories, settings and accessed documents.

Starting A series of two more text characters.

Start-Up Disk A floppy disk which holds the operating system and system configuration files which can, in case of hard disk failure, be used to start the computer.

S

Static RAM Static RAM is also volatile but as long as they are supplied with power, they need no special regenerator circuits to retain the stored data. The static RAM consists eventually of internal flip-flops that store the binary information. The stored information remains valid as long as power is applied to the unit.

Static Variable A variable whose size is determined at compile time and cannot be changed at run time. To use the array of records representation for a linked list, we must estimate the maximum size of the list and declare an array of that size. Even when the list is empty, the array that holds the list uses as much memory as it would if the list were of the maximum size.

Status Bar A line at the top or bottom of a screen which gives information about the task currently being worked on, such as the position of cursor, the number of lines, filename, time and so on.

Statutory Information It consists of reports to be sent to government by law.

STD State-Transition Diagram indicates how the system behaves as a consequence of external events. The STD represents the various modes of behavior (called states) of the system and the manner in which transitions are made from state to state.

Storage Manager Is a program module that provides the interface between the low level data stored in the database and application program and queries submitted to the system. The storage manager is responsible for interaction with the data stored on disk.

Strategic Information It is needed for long range planning. It is less structured and difficult to obtain by processing raw data.

Strong Entity Set	An entity set that has a primary key.
Structured Programming	Any of a number of systems for organized and writing a computer programs so as to reduce the chance for misinterpretation or error.
Sub-Directory	A directory of disk or tape contents contained within another directory.
Sub-Menu	A secondary menu displayed as a choice from a menu. Used if there are too many choices to fit into one menu. A good example is the start button menu which has several submenus for the program and settings menu option.
Sum-Of-Products (SOP)	A sum of products expression is a product term (minterm) or several product terms (minterms) logically added (OR-ed) together.
Sum-Squared Error	Sum of squared differences between the network targets and actual outputs for a given input vector or set of vectors.
Super Key	Is a set of one or more attributes that, taken collectively, allows us to identify uniquely on entity in the entity set.
Super Key	If we add additional attributes to a primary key, the resulting combination would still uniquely identify as record of the entity set. Such augmented keys are called super keys. A primary key is a minimum super key.
Supervised Learning	Learning process in which changes in a network's weights and biases are due to the intervention of any external teacher. The teacher typically provides output targets.
Supportability	It combines the ability to extend the program (extensibility), adaptability, and serviceability as well as testability, compatibility, configurability, the ease with which a system can be installed, and the ease with which problems can be localized.

Swapping At intervals determined by the o.s, usually dictated by cup scheduling policies, jobs are copied from main memory to a backing store and later copied back to main memory. This scheme allows more jobs to be run can be first into memory at one time

Switch A switch forwards each incoming packet only to that port that provides access to the destination system

Switched Off To exit windows select the start/shutdown menu option. With some new PCs, this will also automatically switch off the PC. With older PCs you need to wait until the screen tells you it's safe to switch off the PC.

System A general term that refers to a computer, to a computer and its associated peripherals or to the operating system software such as Windows.

System Analyst Who designs an information system? A system analyst must, through discussions with users, determine their information requirements, interact with them during the design phase and explain to them what the system will provide. He must assign priorities among different requirements, analyze and evaluate existing systems and improve them. An analyst must be able to identify and solve management problems in organizations, draw up specifications and oversee implementation. An analyst should evaluate the designed system and modify them if needed.

A good system analyst must know the operation and management structure of diverse organizations, must understand both hardware and software features of computers, must exhibit good interpersonal relations, be able to express his thoughts well, and capable of life-long learning.

A system analyst should know the use of tools such as DFD, Decision tables, Prototyping systems, Spreadsheets, Database systems, Report generators and Graphics systems.

System Bus The system bus is a communication path between the microprocessor and peripherals; it is nothing but a group of wires to carry bits.

System Design It is concerned with how system functionality to be provided by different components of a system. It involves great deal of feedback and iteration between stages in this process. It also involves deciding which system capabilities are to be implemented in software and which in hardware. System design involves following activities

Partition requirements: there are several partitioning options and a number of alternatives may be produced in this stage.

Identify sub-systems: Identifying sub-systems is carried out along with requirements partitioning. This process is also influenced by organization or environment factors. It is also important to identify hardware to be built.

Assign requirements to sub-systems: Theoretically assigning requirements to subsystems is a straight forward process if requirement partitioning is used to subsystem identification.

Specify subsystem functionality: This phase is a part of system design or sub-system development, or part of requirement specification for it.

Define subsystem interfaces: The interfaces that are provided and expected by each sub-system are defined in this phase. Once it is done, parallel development of subsystem becomes possible.

S

System Development Life Cycle (SDLC)

The SDLC helps you to define the "What", workout the "How" and develop and deliver a quality product by the "When". System development as defined in the SDLC consists of 7 phases as follows

Phase 1: Capturing the Requirements: - Involves sitting down with the client and doing a lot of listening, followed by a lot of writing. The end result is a document that defines what the customer requires in terms that the customer can understand.

Phase 2: Analyzing the requirements: - Involves developing a deeper understanding of the requirements and gather as much data about them as we can, to help us to design a solution.

Phase 3: Designing a solution: - Defines how the product will be built.

Phase 4: Developing a solution: - From what and the how, the individual self-contained modules that make up the solution, is product and tested.

Phase 5: System Integration and Testing: - All the modules developed in phase 4 are taken and put them together as a complete solution. We confirm that we have a solid product that meets all the original requirements.

Phase 6: Implementation and customer acceptance: - the solution is implemented and proved to meet the original requirements.

Phase 7: Support and Maintenance: - After the customer accepts the software, we support and maintain it. This is a final phase of the life cycle.

System Program	A system program is a program which aids in effective execution of a general user's computational requirements on a computer system. System programming is the activity of designing and implementation system program.
System Programming Languages	System programs are designed to make the computer easier to use. An example of system software is an operating system, which consists of many other programs for controlling input / output devices, memory, processor etc. to write an operating system, the programmer needs instruction to control the computer's circuitry (hardware parts).
System Software	The program that control the operation of a computer and all of its peripherals.

T

Tab — To arrange text in columns with the cursor running from one column to the text.

In Windows, a method of moving from one button or field to another without using the mouse, but by pressing the tab key to move the focus.

Tactical Information — It is used to take short range decisions and for better control of the functioning of the organization. It requires complex and ingenious processing of data.

Tapped Delay Line — Sequential set of delays with outputs available at each delay output.

Target Vector — Desired output vector for a given input vector.

Taskbar — A bar that normally runs along the bottom of the screen in Windows 95 and displays the start button and a list of other programs or Windows that are currently active. You can move the entire taskbar to any of the four sides of the screen by clicking on the bar and dragging it to another edge.

TCP/IP — TCP/IP stands for Transmission Control Protocol/Interface Program. A set of standard commands used in networks and the internet to allow computers to exchange information.

TCP/IP Stack — To properly use the TCP/IP protocol, PCs require a TCP/IP stack. This consist of TCP/IP software, sockets software (such as WINSOC.DLL for Windows machines), and hardware (known as packet drivers).

Team Leaders — project management is a people-intensive activity, and for this reason, competent practitioners often make poor team leaders. Weinberg suggests that successful project leaders apply a problem solving management style.

Telecommunication Communicating with other people through the computer using communication software and modems.

Telecommuting Using computers for telecommunication; computer networking.

Teleconferencing To link video, audio and computer signals from different locations so that distant people can talk and see each other.

Telnet The internet standard protocol to connect to remote terminals. Telnet clients are available for most platforms. When you Telnet to a UNIX site, for example, you can issue commands at the prompt as if the machine were local.

Template A template is a file containing standard section of text, such as a memo or invoice, into which specific details such as company address or price can be added.

Terminal A device connected to a computer network that acts as a point for entry or retrieval of information. Personal computer can be made to act as network terminals, by running terminal emulation (communication) programmers.

Terminal Adopter A device, which processes signals coming into a computer from a telecommunication system. Such as device used on analog phone lines is a modem.

Test Case Design The design of tests for software is as challenging as the initial design of the product itself. Yet software engineers often treat testing as an afterthought, developing test cases that may "feel right", but have little assurance of being complete. Test must be that they have the highest likelihood of find the most errors with a minimum amount of time and effort.

T

Test Vectors — Set of input vectors (not used directly in training) that is used to test the trained network.

Testing Objectives — Testing is a process of executing a program with the intent of finding an error

A good test case is one that has high probability of finding an as-yet undiscovered error.

A successful test is one that uncovers an as-yet undiscovered error.

Text File — A file stored on disk that contains text rather than graphics or data.

Text-Dependent (Fixed Password) — The utterance presented to the recognizer is known beforehand. It is based on the assumption that the speaker is cooperative. This is the one that easier to implement, and with higher accuracy.

Text-Independent (Non-Specified Password) — In this condition, the content of speech is unknown. In other words, no assumptions about the text being spoken are made. This is the one that harder to implement, but with higher flexibility.

Thesaurus — A file which contains a collection of synonyms that are displayed as alternative to a mis-spelt word when running a spell check. Also provides a useful vocabulary guide when composing letters or any other type of document.

Theta Notation - θ — $F(n) = \theta\,(g(n))$ iff these exist positive constants C_1 ,C_2 & n_0 such that for all $n > n_0$, $C_1\,|g(n)| \leq |f(n)| \leq C_2[g(n)]$.

Third Normal Form — A relation R is said to be in 3NF if and only if it is in 2NF and every non-key attribute in non-transitively dependent upon the primary key.

THRASHING A process is thrashing if it is spending more time paging than executing. Very high paging activity is called thrashing. It can cause severe performance problems.

Thread A conference topic with multiple responses or a sequence of e-mail messages with the same subject.

Thumbnail A miniature graphical representation of an image. Used by graphic designers as a quick and convenient method of viewing the contents of graphics or DTP files before they are retrieved.

TIFF (TIF, Tagged Image File Format) Stands for tag image file format. A standard file format used to store graphic images (developed by Aldus and Microsoft) that can handle monochrome, grey-scale, 8-bit or 24-bit color image.

There have been many different version of TIFF that include several different compression algorithms

Time Division Multiplexing (TDM) The basic of TDM is the sampling theorem which states that a signal containing frequency components less than f_{max} can be entirely determined by its equidistant samples taken at the rate f_s such that $f_s \geq 2f_{max}$

Time Out What happens when two computers are taking and one fails to respond within a certain time, for whatever reason?

Title Bar A horizontal bar at the top of a window, which displayed the title of the window or of the application.

Toggle Using one command or keystroke to change between one mode and its opposite.

Toolbar A window that contains a range of icon that allows you to access different tools. For example, paint program normally have a toolbar that includes different icons for colors, brush, circle, text and eraser tools. A floating toolbar is a movable window that can be positioned anywhere on screen.

Tooltips A feature of Windows that displays a line of descriptive text under an icon when you move the pointer over that particular icon.

Topic In a conference, a message which is generally written to convey a new idea or a new piece of information, relevant to that conference.

Topology Functions Ways to arrange the neurons in a grid, box, hexagonal, or random topology.

TOUCH PANELS It allows displayed objects or screen positions to be selected with the touch of a finger. Optical touch panels employ a line of infrared light –emitting diodes (LEDS) along one vertical edge and along horizontal edge of the frame.

Touch Screen A computer displays which has a grid of infra-red transmitters and receivers, positioned on either side of the screen, and which is used to control a cursor position. When you want to make a selection to move the cursor, you point to the screen, breaking two of the beams, which give the exact position of your finger.

Traceability The ability to trace a design representation or actual program component back to requirements.

Track Ball The track ball has a ball which can be rotated by hand in any direction. The cursor moves accordingly. It is normally used in medical computers like brain and body scanners etc.

Trackball A device, similar in function to a mouse, but with a fixed base holding a sphere that is manipulated to move the cursor. Some trackballs are mounted on or near the keyboard, especially in laptops or notebook computer.

Training	Procedure whereby a network is adjusted to do a particular job. Commonly viewed as an offline job, as opposed to an adjustment made during each time interval, as is done in adaptive training.
Training	The degree to which the software assist in enabling new users to apply the system.
Training Vector	Input and/or target vector used to train a network.
Transaction Manager	Is responsible for ensuring that the database remains in a consistent (correct) state despite system failure. The transaction manager also ensures that concurrent transaction execution proceed without conflicting.
Transfer Function	Function that maps a neurons (or layer's) net output n to its actual output.
Transformations	The basic geometric transformations arc translation, rotation and sealing. Other transformations that are often applied to objects include reflection and shear.
Trapezoidal Distortion	Distortion of the image on computer screen characterized by sides of the image that are not parallel, or out of square.
Tree	A tree is a non-linear data structure, in a tree structure, each node may point to another node (which may then point to several other nodes etc.) thus tree is a powerful and very flexible data structure that can be used in a variety of applications.
Troubleshoot	To attempt to locate the source of a hardware and software problem and correct it.
Truetype	An outline fount technology introduced by Apple and Microsoft as a means of printing exactly what is displayed on screen. The

technology is also capable of producing fonts that can be scaled to any point size while still remaining smooth.

TSR (Terminate And Stay Resident) A program features, such as a pop-up note pad, that remains stored in RAM when not in use, available to be called up in the active window as needed.

Tuning Phase Period of SOFM training during which weights are expected to spread out relatively evenly over the input space while retaining their topological order found during the ordering phase.

Turning Machine It has a tap that is unbounded in both directions, allowing any number of left and right moves.

It is deterministic in the sense that and defines at most one move for each configuration.

There is no special input file. We assume that at the initial time the tap has some specified content. Some of this may be considered input. Similarly, there is no special output device. Whenever the machine halts, some or all of the contents of the tape may be viewed as output.

TWAIN The standard protocol for scanning images.

Twisted Pair A twisted pair consists of two insulated copper wires, typically about 1 mm thick. The wires are twisted together in a helical form, just as a DNA molecule. The twisted form is used to reduce electrical interference to similar pairs close by.

Types Of Information's Information requirements for managing organizations may be classified as Statutory information, Strategic information, Tactical information and Operational information.

U

UART(Universal Asynchronous Receiver/ Transmitter)	A chip that translates incoming data for the computer& modifies outgoing data for effective transmission.
Unbundled	Descriptive of the availability of an individual software program that is also sold as part of a package such as a draw or paint program that is usually a part of a desktop publishing application.
Underdetermined System	System that has more variables than constraints.
Undo	Functions of some applications that will let you undo the command that you've just carried out. For example, it can undo a paste or a delete operation.
Uninterruptible Power Supply	A sophisticated backup power supply that automatically furnishes battery power to a computer system when the primary power source is interrupted, permitting continued operation or an orderly shutdown.
Unix	A multi-user, multi –tasking operating system developed by AT&T bell laboratories to run on almost any computer, from a PC, to minicomputers and large mainframe. There are a number of graphical user interfaces available, such as open look that hide the Unix command line.
Unsupervised Learning	Learning process in which changes in a network's weights and biases are not due to the intervention of any external teacher. Commonly changes are a function of the current network input vectors, output vectors, and previous weights and biases.

U

Update	Make a change in weights and biases. The update can occur after presentation of a single input vector or after accumulating changes over several input vectors.
Upgrade	To improve the performance or specification of your computer by adding more RAM ,a larger hard disk or another kind of improvement .software can also be upgraded from an old version to a more recent one.
Uptime	The period when a computer is on line & functioning property.
URL	stands for uniform resource locator. Internet system used to standard the way in which world wide web addresses is written.
Usability	Is assessed by considering human factors, overall architect, consistencies and documentation .
USB Universal Serial Bus	A serial "information path "through which the CPU communicates with device such as scanners. USB ports are being used on newer device instead of the older COM ports. USB devices can be used on both IBM clones and Macs.
Usenet	Usenet groups are more commonly known as newsgroups. There are thousands of groups hosted on hundreds of servers around the world, dealing with various topics. News reader software is required to properly download and view articles in the groups, but you can usually post an article to a group simply by emailing to it.

User Friendly A description of software which is easy to use particularly for novice or Inexperienced computer user.

User Interface Software which operates between the user and the operating system, often to make the latter easier to use.

Utterance Spoken input from the user of a speech application. An utterance may be a single word, an entire phrase, a sentence, or even several sentences.

V

V.32, V.32Bis, V.42, V.42Bis	Error –correction and data compression protocols that make modems communicate more quickly and reliably.
VAFC VESA Advanced Feature Connector	A type of video bus architecture for displaying video images on a computer monitor screen.
Validation Vectors	Set of input vectors (not used directly in training) that is used to monitor training progress so as to keep the network from over fitting.
Vector Graphics, Image	1) a system of drawing objects using curves and lines. The images are described by line length and direction from an origin to plot lines and build up an image rather than a description of each pixel, as in a bitmap image.
Vector Quantization (VQ)	It's a quantization technique used to compress the information and manipulate the data such in a way to maintain the most prominent characteristics. VQ is used in many applications such as data compression (i.e. image and voice compression), voice recognition, etc.
Veronica	**Veronica** was a search engine system for the Gopher protocol, developed in 1992 by Steven Foster and Fred Barrie at the University of Nevada, Reno. During its existence, Veronica was a constantly updated database of the names of almost every menu item on thousands of Gopher servers. The Veronica database could be searched from most major Gopher menus. Although the original Veronica database is no longer accessible, various local Veronica installations and at least one complete rewrite ("Veronica-2") still exist.

VESA (Video Electronics Standards Association) A trade organization formed mainly to standardize graphics display modes for computer monitors.

Vesa Local Bus A 32-bit local bus standard that enables communication directly with a processor at its rated CPU clock speed.

VGA Stands for graphics array. A standard of video adapter developed by IBM that can support a display with a resolution up to 640*480 pixels in 256 colors. Superseded by SVGA which is an enhancement to the standard VGA graphics display system that allows resolutions of up to 800* 600 pixels in 16 million colors.

Video –Conferencing To link two or more computers that can capture and display video and audio in real time so that distant people can talk and see each other.

Video Digitizers A high-speed digital sampling circuit, which stores a TV, picture in memory so that a pc can then process it.

Video For Windows Abbreviated to VFW. Set of software drivers and utilities for Microsoft windows 3.1that allows AVI format video files to be played back in a window. Video for windows supports several compression methods including Microsoft video 1, Microsoft RLE and Intel index. Once the video for windows driver is installed, video clips can be played back using the windows media player utility.

Video Game A game played on a PC that can be either an adventure game where you have to explore an electronic world or an arcade game in which you have to shoot lots of baddies.

Video Graphics Card An expansion card that fits into an expansion slot inside your PC and allows it to display text and graphics and moving video images from an external camera or VCR.

Video Memory (VRAM) A section of memory fitted on a video adapter that is used as a temporary store for image data sent from the PC's main memory or to store an image as it is built up and before it is displayed on the screen.

Virtual Something which does not actually exist, expect in an imaginary form in a computer.

Virtual Hashing In contrast to any known hashing, a virtual hashing may modify its hashing function. Such changes may be performed when collisions arise. A virtual hashing may then find in one disk access, a record such that several accesses would be needed if the function initially chosen for the file was used. We define virtual hashing's which practically independently of the number of such records find in one disk access almost each record of the file.

Virtual Image A complete image stored in memory rather than the part of it that is displayed.

Virtual Memory A set of technique that allow us to execute Program which is not entirely in memory. Demand paging is the Common virtual memory system.

Virtual Memory A large imaginary main memory which is made available to an operating system by storing unused parts of the virtual memory on disk and then transferring these pages into available main memory as and they are required.

Virtual Reality Abbreviated to VR . a simulation of a real-life scene or environment by a computer, which you can interact with and explore.

Virtual Storage Access Method (VSAM)

The term VSAM applies to both a data set type and the access method used to manage various user data types. As an access method, VSAM provides much more complex functions than other disk access methods. VSAM keeps disk records in a unique format that is not understandable by other access methods. VSAM is used primarily for applications. It is not used for source programs, JCL, or executable modules. VSAM files cannot be routinely displayed or edited with ISPF. You can use VSAM to organize records into four types of data sets: key-sequenced, entry-sequenced, linear, or relative record. The primary difference among these types of data sets is the way their records are stored and accessed.

Virus

A computer virus is an insidious piece of software that infects other Software and moves from computer to computer when software is transferred. A virus may compound itself once it's inside your computer, thereby destroying software programs and a great deal of data or it may do other nasty things. Some viruses are benign. Modems can transmit viruses, but illegally copied or diskettes are the most likely carriers. Virus protection software is the best defense, and is available commercially or as freeware/shareware.

Vocabulary

The total list of words the speech engine will be comparing an utterance against. The vocabulary is made up of all the words in all active grammars. The size of vocabulary of a speech recognition system affects the complexity, processing requirements and the accuracy of the system. Some applications only require a few words (e.g. numbers only), others require very large dictionaries (e.g.

dictation machines). There are no established definitions, however, try

small vocabulary - tens of words

medium vocabulary - hundreds of words

large vocabulary - thousands of words

very-large vocabulary - tens of thousands of words.

Voice Recognition A form of biometrics that identifies users by recognizing their unique voices. Though it is often used interchangeably with speech recognition, the two are different. Voice recognition is concerned with recognizing voices, while speech recognition is concerned with recognizing the content of speech.

Vt100 A terminal-type setting with this setting a network system assumes you are using a VT100 terminal or a computer program that acts like one.

W

WAIS (Wide Area Information Service) A distributed information service and search engine that allows natural language input and indexed searching . Many web search utilities use a WAIS engine.

Wallpaper In windows, an image or pattern used as a background in a window. You can change the wallpaper to windows from within the control panel/desktop icon setting.

Warm Boot A restart of a computer system while it is running and without turning off the system, often occasioned by a program or hardware malfunction that locks up the system or causes it to perform erratically.

Waterfall Model This model has five phases: the developer must complete each phase before the next phase begins. This model is named " waterfall model", because its diagrammatic representation resembles a cascade of waterfalls. The various phases are:

Requirement analysis and Specification phase

Design phase

Implementation and unit testing phase

Integration and system testing phase

Operation and maintenance phase

Wave To Wave File A standard method of storing an analog signal in digital form under Microsoft windows

Weak Entity Set An entity set may not have sufficient attributes to form a primary key. Such an entity set is termed a weak entity set.

Weight Balanced Trees A **weight-balanced binary tree** is a binary tree which is balanced based on knowledge of the probabilities of searching for each individual node. Within each subtree, the node with the highest weight appears at the root. This can result in more efficient searching performance.

Weight Function Weight functions apply weights to an input to get weighted inputs, as specified by a particular function.

Weight Matrix Matrix containing connection strengths from a layer's inputs to its neurons. The element $W_{i,j}$ of a weight matrix W refers to the connection strength from input j to neuron i.

Weighted Input Vector Result of applying a weight to a layer's input, whether it is a network input or the output of another layer.

White Box Testing Sometimes called glass-box testing, is a test case design method that uses the control structure of the procedural design to derive test cases . test cases

Guarantee that all independent paths within a module have been exercised at least once

Exercise all logical decisions on their true and false sides

Execute all loops at their boundaries and within their operational founds.

Exercise internal data structures to assure their validity.

White Pages Databases containing email addresses, telephone numbers, and postal addresses of internet users. You can search the internet white pages to find information about particular users.

WHOIS An internet program (related to finger and the white pages) that lets you enter an internet entity (such as domains, networks, and hosts) and display information such as a person's company name, address, phone number and email address.

Wide Area Information Servers (WAIS) It is a client-server text searching system that uses the ANSI Standard Z39.50 Information Retrieval Service Definition and Protocol Specifications for Library Applications" (Z39.50:1988) to search index databases on remote computers. It was developed in the late 1980s as a project of Thinking Machines, Apple Computer, Dow Jones, and KPMG Peat Marwick. WAIS did not adhere to either the standard or its OSI framework (adopting instead TCP/IP) but created a unique protocol inspired by Z39.50:1988.

Widrow-Hoff Learning Rule Learning rule used to train single-layer linear networks. This rule is the predecessor of the back propagation rule and is sometimes referred to as the delta rule.

Wildcards A symbol used when searching for files or data which represents all files; in DOS, UNIX, and PC operating systems, the wild card character '?' will match any single character in this position. The wild card character "or" means match any number of any characters.

Windows A multi-tasking graphical user interface for the IBM PC developed by Microsoft that is designed to be easy to use. Windows uses icons to represent files and devices and can be controlled using a mouse, unlike MS-DOS, which requires commands to be typed. Or, in simple words, a rectangular viewing area on a computer monitor screen where data is displayed.

Windows 3.1 The first of the new generation of windows which provided features including OLE and drag and drop.

Windows 3.11 The official version number for windows for workgroups.

W

Windows Explorer A software utility included with windows 95, which allows you to view the folders and files on your hard disk, floppy disk, CD-ROM and any shared network drives.

Windows For Workgroups A version of windows that includes the functions that let you connects several computers together to form a network and share files, printers and exchange data. It also includes software for email, fax and scheduler utilities.

Windows NT A high-performance program derived from windows, which provides a robust, fast operating system for network workstations or for the central server in a network.

Windows9x Another name for window 98.

Winsocks Stands for windows sockets. Winsocks is a set of specifications or standards for programmers creating TPC/IP applications for use with windows.

Wirfs –Brock Method It doesn't make a clear distinction between analysis and design tasks, instead, a continuous process that begins with the assessment of a customer specification and with design is proposed.

Word The word (or word length) is defined as the number of bits the microprocessor recognizes and processes at a time. The word length ranges from four bits for small, microprocessor-based systems to 64 bits for high speed large computers.

Word Pad A software utility included with windows 95 that provides the basic functions of Microsoft word 6. . it can read and save word 6 files and lets you format text and write complex documents.

Word Processor A program used to enter or edit text information in personal computers, often used to create a file before it is uploaded to a network; may also be used to process text after it has been downloaded.

Workstations The workstations are designed around RISC (Reduced Instruction Set Computing) processors. The RISC processors tend to be faster and more efficient than the processors used in personal computers.

World Wide Web (www) Abbreviated to www. Within the internet, thousands of pages of formatted text and graphics (stored in HTML) that allow a user to have a graphical user interface to the internet rather than a less user –friendly command –line interface.

Worm Stands for write once, read many times memory. An optical disc storage system that allows the user to write data to the disc once. The user can then read the data from the disc many times.

WYSIWYG "what you see is that you get". A word processing or DTP program where what you see on the screen is exactly the same as the image or text that be printed, including graphics and special fonts.

X

XLS	File name extension for a spread file.
XML: Extensible Markup Language.	It is a format of exchanging data. This format is not owned by any organization, but is accepted by a host of companies as a standard for data interchange. XML facilities moving structured data across the web by being independent of system or platform restrictions. XML is a transmission format of B2B and B2C because it enables information exchange and makes it easy to publish report information on numerous platforms and devices.
Xmodem	A communications protocol that allows you to transfer files between your computer and a network with error correction.
XT	The original version of the IBM PC, developed by IBM that used an 8088 processor and included a hard disk.
XT Keyboard	A type of keyboard used by the IBM PC, which had ten function keys running in two columns along the left –hand side of the keyboard. The current standard is called the AT or windows 95 keyboard . these included 12 function key and, in the case of a windows 95 keyboard, a special button that's equivalent to pressing the start button on screen.

Y

YACC YACC stands for Yet Another Compiler Compiler. It assists in the next phase of the compiler. It creates a parser which will be output in a form suitable for inclusion in the next phase. Yacc is available as a command (utility) on the UNIX system and has been used to help implement hundreds of compilers.

YAHOO Yet another hierarchic officious oracle.

YIQ Color Model The National television system committee (NTSC) Color model for forming the composite video signal is the YIQ Model, which is based on concepts in the CIEXYZ model.

Z

ZAP	A program command to clear a monitor screen and start fresh To unintentionally delete or overwrite a computer file.
Zero Insertion Force Socket	Abbreviated to ZIF. A socket that has movable connection terminals, allowing the chips to be inserted without using any force. A small lever is turned to grip the legs of the chip. ZIF sockets are used to hold chips inside your computer, making it easier to replace or upgrade the processor.
Zero Wait State	An electronic device (normally a processor or memory chips) that is fast enough to turn at the same speed as the other components in a computer, so does not have to be artificially slowed down by inserting wait states.
Zmodem	Another error-checking file transfer protocol faster than or Kermit.
Zoom	To enlarge an area of text or graphics to make it easier to see or work on.